GREENE

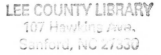

MILITARY PROFILES
SERIES EDITOR
Dennis E. Showalter, Ph.D.
Colorado College

*Instructive summaries for general and
expert readers alike, volumes in the
Military Profiles series are essential
treatments of significant and popular
military figures drawn from world history,
ancient times through the present.*

GREENE

Revolutionary General

Steven E. Siry

Potomac Books, Inc.
Washington, D.C.

Library of Congress Cataloging-in-Publication Data
Siry, Steven E., 1956–
   Greene : revolutionary general / Steven E. Siry.—1st ed.
     p. cm.—(Military profiles)
   Includes bibliographical references and index.
ISBN 1-57488-912-5 (hardcover : alk. paper)—ISBN 1-57488-913-3 (pbk. : alk. paper)
1. Greene, Nathanael, 1742–1786. 2. Generals—United States—Biography. 3. United States. Continental Army—Biography. 4. United States—History—Revolution, 1775–1783—Campaigns.
I. Title. II. Series.

E207.G9S57 2006
973.3'3092—dc22 [B]

                             2006001587

ISBN-10 1-57488-912-5 HC
ISBN-13 978-1-57488-912-3 HC
ISBN-10 1-57488-913-3 PB
ISBN-13 978-1-57488-913-0 PB

Printed in the United States of America on acid-free paper that meets the American National Standards Institute Z39-48 Standard.

Potomac Books, Inc.
22841 Quicksilver Drive
Dulles, Virginia 20166

First Edition

10 9 8 7 6 5 4 3 2 1

For my wife, Hairani, and my daughters, Aleah and Nadira
—*so precious and so loved.*

"We are Soldiers who devote ourselves to arms not for the invasion of other Countries but for the defence of our own; not for the gratification of our own private Interest, but for the Public Security. Nevertheless they that assume this Character and possess a happy Genius accompanyed with a prudent conduct, and fortune smiles on their endeavors, they have an Opportunity of traveling the shortest Road to the greatest heights of Ambition, and may the deserving obtain what their merit entitles them to."

General Nathanael Greene
July 14, 1775

"I trust history will do justice to the reputations of individuals."

General Nathanael Greene
July [25?], 1778

Contents

Maps

As Nathanael Greene grew to manhood in a Quaker family, it seemed very unlikely that he would eventually embark on a military career. However, the deterioration in Anglo-American relations in the early 1770s motivated Greene to defend America's liberties against what he believed were tyrannical actions by the British government that threatened to impose political slavery on the American colonists. After abandoning the Society of Friends' belief in pacifism, Greene's total military training to mid-1775 consisted of serving as a private in the Rhode Island militia for a few hours each week. And because of a slight limp, he was passed over when officers were elected. Thus it remains a mystery why the Rhode Island assembly in May 1775 appointed Greene as commander of the Rhode Island Army of Observation at the siege of Boston. Moreover, the following month, at age thirty-two, he became the youngest general in the Continental Army. His rise to leadership had been meteoric. Eight years later he was the only one of George Washington's generals to have served continuously throughout the Revolutionary War.

Resourceful and courageous, Greene also combined a keen intellect, unyielding determination, fine organizational skills, and a remarkable aptitude for using geographical information. Learning his craft and developing leadership skills as the war progressed, Greene became Washington's most trusted advisor. Although a sense of duty was central to his service, this was intertwined with his desire for enduring heroic fame from military glory. And he relentlessly worked to establish an outstanding reputation as a citizen-soldier of the new republic.

After distinguishing himself in the northern campaign and providing invaluable service as quartermaster general for more than two years, Greene became commander of the Southern Department with orders to rebuild its forces following the loss of two American armies in South Carolina in 1780. The situation seemed hopeless, since Georgia and South Carolina were under British control and North Carolina and Virginia appeared open to an enemy invasion. Indeed, the Rhode Islander found himself in a situation that could destroy the reputation he had worked so hard to create.

Greene, however, combined regulars, militia, and guerrillas into a very effective force that used rapid movement and continuous pressure against the British. More than any other general in the Continental Army during the Revolutionary War, he employed partisan forces as a critical part of an overall strategy against the enemy. In fact, his great innovation was coordinating the movements of regular and partisan troops in an extremely mobile type of warfare, which frequently exchanged space for time while waiting for an opportunity to engage in full-scale battle. Greene, therefore, was a revolutionary general in a twofold sense. Besides his military position in the War of Independence, he developed a strategy of unconventional war that foreshadowed aspects of the irregular warfare used in many later conflicts of national liberation.

Initially dividing his army in the face of a numerically superior enemy, Greene recaptured the strategic initiative. Eventually reuniting his army, he changed the American situation in the lower South by outmaneuvering the enemy commanders. After suffering heavy losses, British forces by 1782 were restricted to just two seaports in the South, which greatly aided the rebel cause as the Americans won their War of Independence. Greene had developed and superbly filled the role of an innovative general who maintained his army and greatly restricted the area of British control. As a result, Greene did more than protect his reputation; he elevated it to a new level that would place him among the most revered in Revolutionary America's pantheon of heroic leaders.

Greene, however, would have little time to enjoy the laurels of his military success. Burdened by great financial debts incurred during the war, he struggled for three years after the conflict to provide for his family by attempting to make plantations awarded to him by grateful southern state legislatures into productive estates. But he would die at age forty-three before he could reverse his financial situation.

During his incomplete life, Greene had traveled far, and he had been transformed by the journey. He abandoned his Quaker beliefs and became a soldier, as he also ended his loyalty to the British crown and became a leading revolutionary. Furthermore, during the war his views on strategy evolved to include an emphasis on unconventional warfare. All of these changes occurred as Greene's sense of personal and national mission motivated him to become one of the most important architects of the American victory in the War for Independence.

In writing this brief military biography of Greene I have drawn on the work of many scholars. I am especially indebted to the editors of *The Papers of General Nathanael Greene*, who during the last thirty years have produced thirteen superb volumes of Greene's letters. This excellently annotated compilation is essential for writing a biography of the Rhode Islander. Moreover, I am grateful to Rick Russell, an editor and the associate publisher at Potomac Books, and Dr. Dennis Showalter, the editor of the "Military Profiles" series, for helping to carry this work through to completion. Finally, I wish to thank the three ladies who are so special to me: my wife, Hairani, and my daughters, Aleah and Nadira.

Steven E. Siry
Kuala Lumpur, Malaysia

Chronology

1778	Leads troops at the Battle of Monmouth Courthouse on June 28.
1778	Commands the right wing at the Battle of Rhode Island on August 29.
1780	Resigns as quartermaster general on July 26.
1780	In September, presides over the military court that sentences John André to hang for acting as a spy in aiding Benedict Arnold's treasonous efforts to surrender the fort at West Point.
1780	Appointed as commander at West Point in early October.
1780	On October 14 is chosen to command the Continental Army in the Southern Department.
1780	On December 16 decides to divide his army in the Carolinas.
1781	On March 15 leads his army at the Battle of Guilford Courthouse.
1781	Commands his army at the Battle Hobkirk's Hill on April 25.
1781	From May 22 through June 19 directs unsuccessful siege at Ninety-Six.
1781	On September 8 leads his army at the Battle of Eutaw Springs.
1782	In December occupies Charleston after its evacuation by the British.
1783	In June furloughs the Southern Army, and on November 27 is reunited with his family in Newport, Rhode Island.
1785	Settles on a large plantation near Savannah, Georgia, that was given to him by the state.
1786	Dies at his plantation on June 19.

GREENE

Beginnings (1742–74)

Nathanael Greene was born on July 27, 1742, to a wealthy Quaker family at Potowomut (now Warwick), Rhode Island. His family's history stretched back to nearly the start of permanent English settlements in New England. He was a descendant of John Greene, a surgeon, who had emigrated from England to America in the 1630s for religious reasons. John Greene was a follower of Roger Williams, who was exiled from Massachusetts Bay because of his religious beliefs. Greene moved with Williams to the area that became Rhode Island, and in the early 1640s Greene and several other religious dissidents purchased land from the Wampanoag Indians, which became the township of Potowomut. John Greene's son, James, later purchased a sizeable amount of land between Potowomut Creek and Greenwich Bay. James's son, Jabez Greene, in 1684 built a family homestead on the site, and this was where Nathanael Greene was born.

Greene was the fifth of a family of nine children: eight boys and a girl. Three of the children were from his father's first marriage and the rest from a second. Greene's mother, Mary Mott, died when Nathanael was eleven. His father, also named Nathanael, had inherited extensive property, owned an ironworks, and became a very successful businessman.

As a teenager, Greene developed a passion for dancing and parties, which upset his father because this was not in keeping with Quaker beliefs. Family tradition says that Nathanael even occasionally climbed down the woodshed roof from his second-story bedroom to escape the house without his father noticing. Once, however, when he returned from dancing, his father was waiting for him outside the house, whip in hand. Spying his father, Nathanael crept to a stack of cedar shingles nearby and used some to pad his breeches. The whipping therefore did not have the desired effect, though his yells of pain were quite convincing.

Greene noted that his father was "a man [of] great Piety, . . . and was govern'd in his conduct by Humanity and kind Benevolence. But his mind was overshadow'd with prejudices against Literary Accomplishments." This meant that, "very early when I should have been in the pursuit of Knowledge, I was digging into the Bowels of the Earth after wealth." Greene further asserted, "I lament the want of a liberal Education; I feel the mist [of] Ignorance to surround me, for my own part I was Educated a Quaker, and amongst the most Supersticious sort, and that of its self is a sufficient Obstacle to cramp the best of Geniuses, much more [than] mine." Nevertheless, Greene convinced his father to hire a tutor named Adam Maxwell, who was a Scot residing in East Greenwich. He taught Greene geometry and some Latin. In addition, besides the Bible, he read the writings of William Penn and other standard Quaker works.[1]

Beginning in his late teens, he also met several men who would help direct his academic development. Among these was Lindley Murray, who was studying law in New York City and many years later became an important grammarian. He encouraged Greene to read law, including William Blackstone's *Commentaries*. This allowed Greene to handle legal matters connected to the family's ironworks, and this association with lawyers and judges in turn led to Greene developing better speaking skills and social graces.

Traveling frequently to Newport on business and legal matters, Greene purchased books at the town's bookstores. He eventually had a library of more than two hundred works on a wide range of topics, including numerous books on military science. In a letter to a friend in 1771, Greene declared that he supported higher education, though this was not in keeping with Quaker doctrine. Influenced by Enlightenment thought, Greene asserted that education should result in "Virtuous Manners. . . [which] lead to a steady Prosecution of the general Welfare of Society: [and] Virtuous Principles . . . as tend to confirm these Habits by Superinduceing the Idea of Duty." This emphasis on duty was to overcome the pursuit of self-interest, which he believed was the primary force of human motivation.[2]

When he reached adulthood, Greene stood five feet ten inches tall, with a muscular upper body that resulted from his work in the family forge. But he had a very slight limp, which was probably due to a congenital condition, and he had suffered from asthma since early childhood. Moreover, in his early twenties he received a smallpox inoculation that caused a fever that affected his right eye. Later in life the eye sometimes became painfully infected. Overall, despite some brief periods of illness, his health during the Revolutionary War would be quite good.

After the death of his half-brother Thomas, Greene inherited land in West Greenwich that made him a freeman at age twenty-one. Although he could now vote at town meetings, he was not particularly interested in local politics. Even Parliament's passage of the 1767 Townshend Duties, which placed revenue-raising taxes on some imports to the American colonies, did not lead to Greene becoming actively involved in opposing Britain's new imperial policy.

In 1770 he became the manager of the family ironworks at Coventry, a village of approximately one hundred families, which was about eight miles west of East Greenwich on the Pawtuxet River. Most of the Coventry men worked at the forge, which was larger than the ironworks owned by the Greene family at Potowomut.

Greene's father died in November 1770, but eight years would pass before Greene and his brothers divided their father's estate. This included the ironworks, which had become a major business in the colony. In addition, the Greenes would invest in several commercial vessels.

In the early 1770s Greene also spent part of each year serving in the Rhode Island legislature. Most of his time, however, was spent in Coventry, where he lived the life of a bachelor. In Coventry Greene built a Georgian-style frame house, called Spell Hall, which had eight rooms divided between two stories. He received many visitors and began to court Hannah Ward, the eldest daughter of Samuel Ward, former two-time governor of Rhode Island who led the southern faction in the colony's politics. But Greene was devastated when she rejected his marriage proposal in the summer of 1772.

Also in 1772 the so-called "Quiet Period" in Anglo-American relations, which began in 1770 with the repeal of all the Townshend Duties except the one on tea, was threatened in Rhode Island by an incident that involved Greene. In February 1772 William Dudingston, captain of the British vessel *Gaspee*, seized one of the Greene family's ships, the *Fortune*, for allegedly being involved in a smuggling operation. The ship was sent to Boston, which Greene asserted was an unlawful infringement of his rights as a Rhode Island citizen. Greene traveled several times to Boston to retrieve his vessel. Dudingston eventually admitted that he had ignored the law in seizing the *Fortune*, and so the court asserted that Dudingston had to pay 295 pounds sterling to the Greenes to cover damages. Nevertheless, Greene remained outraged by Dudingston's actions; indeed, the incident marked a turning point in Greene's view of Anglo-American relations.

Then, in June 1772, a group of Rhode Islanders boarded the *Gaspee*, seriously wounded Dudingston, and set fire to the ship, which burned to the waterline in Narragansett Bay. A Parliamentary act had recently made it a crime punishable by death to burn a ship of the Royal navy. The Privy Council created a secret board of enquiry to find those responsible, but the investigators were unsuccessful in their efforts. Nevertheless, Stephen Hopkins, who served as chief justice on the Superior Court in Rhode Island and was a leader of the resistance to Britain's new imperial policies, informed Greene that one of the *Gaspee*'s officers had claimed Greene was involved in the destruction of the ship. He vehemently denied the charge, saying it had resulted from the practice of offering large rewards for information, which led people to commit perjury. Outraged by the British government's actions, Greene asserted that he feared the "Liberties of the People will be trampled to Death by the Prerogatives of the Crown."[3]

As Greene opposed Britain's new imperial policies, the final stage of the colonial movement toward independence was initiated by a

Parliamentary act to save the nearly bankrupt East India Company, which had vast amounts of tea that it could not sell. The Tea Act of 1773 gave the East India Company the right to ship its tea directly to its North American colonies. Though there would remain a small revenue-raising tax on tea, smuggled Dutch tea would be undersold. If all went as Parliament planned, the East India Company would be saved from bankruptcy, the British government would receive a modest revenue, and the American colonists would be able to purchase inexpensive tea.

Many of the colonists, however, loudly denounced the act. American merchants opposed the East India Company's monopoly, and opponents of Britain's new imperial policies condemned the continuation of a revenue-raising tax. When the tea ships arrived, the Americans responded by dumping 10,000 pounds sterling of the tea in Boston harbor. In response, Parliament attempted to punish the colonists for the Boston Tea Party and to lessen home rule for Massachusetts by passing, in 1774, the Coercive Acts, which Americans soon dubbed the Intolerable Acts. This legislation closed the port of Boston to all commerce until the tea was paid for; disallowed Massachusetts town meetings except for electing town officials; stated that the King, rather than the Massachusetts assembly, would appoint the governor's council; asserted that in order to ensure a fair jury for any British soldier or official accused of a capital crime, any such person could have a change of venue to a location outside of Massachusetts; and allowed the quartering of British troops in private homes as long as a reasonable rent was paid for the housing. These acts alarmed people in all of the colonies since they recognized that the British government could apply such laws in the future to any colony that opposed Britain's new imperial policies.

Americans were additionally alarmed at the passage of the Quebec Act, which tried to keep the loyalty of French Canadians by upholding religious freedom for Catholics in Canada. But the act also asserted that the Quebec government would control the Ohio Valley, a measure intended to stop the movement of land-hungry Americans into the Trans-Appalachian area and thus preserve peace with the Indians. Assessing the situation, Greene declared that he wished the angel who had destroyed Assyrian ruler Sennacherib's army would do the same to the British force in America.

In response to the Coercive Acts and Quebec Act, the colonial legislatures selected delegates to attend a Continental Congress, which met in Philadelphia in September. The Rhode Island legislature chose Samuel Ward and Stephen Hopkins, Greene's friends, as the colony's delegates. Greene was happy with their selection, because he felt they would strongly defend colonial rights. And the Congress subsequently did pass a declaration of grievances that condemned British imperial policies set after 1763. Moreover, the Congress established a new economic boycott of British goods and endorsed the so-called Suffolk Resolves that called for the colonists to arm themselves to defend their liberties.

Less than six weeks before the Continental Congress met, thirty-one-year-old Greene married Catharine Littlefield, who was called Caty and was thirteen years younger than her husband. After a seven-month courtship during which he was much enamored with the attractive, witty, and vivacious niece of Samuel Ward, the two married in the Greene family's old mansion. Following the wedding, they resided at Greene's home in Coventry.

Greene's attention, however, remained partly on the growing crisis between Great Britain and its North American colonies. In late August 1774, Greene and nearly eighty other people signed a subscription list to donate funds to the citizens of Boston who were under "the Late Cruel, malignant and more than savage [Coercive] Acts of the British Parliament."[4]

Since early 1772 Greene had become an ardent opponent of Britain's new imperial policies for the colonies. His sense of duty and his outrage over the British actions regarding the *Fortune* had led him to reject the pacifism of his Quaker upbringing and to prepare for the military defense of America's liberties. Indeed, he stood on the threshold of a meteoric rise within the emerging American military establishment.

Rebellion (1774–76)

T HE BRITISH government could not avoid responding to the Continental Congress's resolutions. The Declaratory Act of 1766 had asserted that the King and Parliament had the authority to pass legislation for the colonies "in all cases whatsoever," and the Coercive Acts and the Quebec Act were an outgrowth of that legislation. Faced with American defiance, the British government could only have avoided conflict with the colonies by opening negotiations to repeal the Coercive Acts. That would not happen, as the British government continued to believe that the defiance in America represented the actions of just a few radical leaders rather than widespread opposition. The British plan was to use military force to uphold the royal standard in the colonies and capture the rabble-rousers. To implement the strategy of military intimidation, Gen. Thomas Gage, the commander in chief of the British army in North America, had assembled a force of 3,500 troops by December 1774.

Meanwhile, groups were meeting throughout New England to create military companies that would complement the colonial militia. Included among these separate forces was the Military Independent Company of East Greenwich, which soon became the Kentish Guards. Greene was very involved in forming this company, which the colonial legislature assigned to a volunteer regiment. Writing to his friend James M. Varnum in late October 1774, he asserted, "I thought the cause of Liberty was in danger and as it was attackt by a military force it was necessary to cultivate a military spirit amongst this People, that should tyranny endeavor to make any farther advances we might be prepared to check it in its first sallies." Greene would later assert that military action was needed for "the preservation of the Rights of Human Nature and the Liberties of America." Indeed, he declared, "[W]e have no alternative but to fight it out or be [political] slaves."[1]

Greene, like many Americans, was influenced by a political ideology that partly came from classical currents of thought, partly drew on Renaissance writings and Enlightenment theories, and partly derived from English opposition groups' "country" ideology. This revolutionary republicanism held that power is always dangerous since those who wield it naturally try to enlarge its scope. This could transform a constitutional government into a tyrannical regime and impose political slavery on the citizenry. It was therefore the duty of citizens to oppose the abuse of power. In fact, many Americans perceived British policies after 1763 as a systematic attack on their natural rights and fundamental Anglo-American liberties. They believed it would take extraordinary virtue in people from all classes of society to resist this tyranny.

During the second half of 1774, Greene traveled several times to Boston. He usually stayed at the Bunch of Grapes Tavern, where other leaders who opposed Britain's new imperial policies also stayed. In Boston Greene, who smuggled a musket out of the town under hay in a wagon, procured the services of a British deserter to train the Kentish Guards three times a week for three months. At that time, another British veteran was also hired to serve as a drillmaster. Moreover, during his stay, Greene watched and learned the British method of drilling, which troops practiced on Boston Common. And he learned aspects of the engineering methods used by the British as they fortified Boston Neck.

Wanting to add more publications on military science to his library, Greene went to Henry Knox's bookstore in Boston. The two men, who would soon be serving together in the Continental Army, discussed defense issues and began to develop a close friendship. Back in Coventry, Greene studied the military manuals and books, and he used the forge to make artillery and cannonballs for Rhode Island's army.

Despite Greene's military knowledge and his efforts on behalf of the Kentish Guards, the barely noticeable limp in his right leg prevented him from being elected as one of the company's officers. Greene wrote to James Varnum, captain of the Guards, "I was informd the Gentlemen of East Greenwich said that I was a blemish to the company. I confess it is the first stroke of mortification that I ever felt from being considered either in private or publick Life a blemish to those with whom I assosiateed." Greene considered resigning from the company, but he eventually decided to stay as a private. His injured pride had succumbed to his sense of duty. Although Greene stayed in the Kentish Guards, he also remained a member of the Quakers' Greenwich Meeting. In fact, he would only sever his ties with the group in 1777.[2]

In February 1775 Parliament declared Massachusetts to be in a state of rebellion. And on April 14 General Gage received orders to use military force against the colony's rebels. Four days later, he dispatched a strike force of seven hundred troops to seize the rebels' supplies at Concord. But rebel horseback riders, including Paul Revere, spread a warning to the countryside about the British march. At dawn on April 19 militiamen met the British strike force at Lexington and then later in the day at Concord. Facing a large number of militiamen at the latter town, the British retreated to Boston, but they were often under fire from the militiamen along the narrow roads. By the end of April 19, seventy-three British soldiers and forty-nine American militiamen were dead. The conflict that started in 1763 over taxes and constitutional issues had finally resulted in open rebellion and civil war.

The Kentish Guards headed to Boston to provide assistance to the Massachusetts militia. At Pawtucket, however, they heard that the British had retreated into Boston; so the Guards returned to Coventry. In response to the fighting at Lexington and Concord, the Rhode Island legislature held a special session beginning on April 22. The assembly created a 1,500-man force, known as the Army of

Observation, to protect America's liberties in the name of King George III against Parliament's army. Clearly the defense of liberty did not yet mean the repudiation of loyalty to the crown. The legislature then chose Private Nathanael Greene to be the brigadier general in command of the Rhode Island army. Why he was selected over dozens of militia officers, including many veterans of the French and Indian War, has been one of the enduring mysteries of the Revolutionary era. Greene's connection to Samuel Ward, a former governor of Rhode Island, was certainly an important factor. Moreover, Greene had served in the legislature, and his brother, Jacob, was a deputy in the legislature and one of five members of Rhode Island's Committee of Safety. Nevertheless, other men had more military experience and better political connections than Greene. It seems that mostly by chance the legislature made a very wise selection. Indeed, Greene's performance in the war undoubtedly would surpass even the assemblymen's greatest expectations.

Before leaving for Massachusetts, Greene began recruiting and training the Army of Observation, and he worked with the Committee of Safety and the Commissary to purchase weapons, munitions, and other supplies. Greene also worked with another committee that created a military code for regulating the new army. After a brief stay in Massachusetts, by late May, Greene was back in Rhode Island because of shortages of supplies for his regiments. Unable to go to Coventry to visit his wife, Greene wrote to her that "the injury done my Country, and the Chains of Slavery forgeing for posterity, calls me fourth to defend our common rights, and repel the bold invaders of the Sons of Freedom. The cause is the cause of God and man. . . . I hope the righteous God that rules the World will bless the Armies of America."[3]

By early June Greene returned to Massachusetts with two of the three regiments of the Army of Observation. The other regiment arrived several weeks later. Soon after his arrival in Massachusetts, Greene met with the commanding generals of armies from other colonies. All of the commanding generals were older than Greene and had more military experience. Nevertheless, it was clear that they had received glowing reports about Greene's ability, and they already recognized that the Rhode Island troops were a cut above other New England troops in order and discipline. "Were I to estimate my value by the attention paid to my opinion," Greene wrote to Caty, "I should have reason to think myself some considerable personage." Since the conflict was in Massachusetts, Greene offered to place the Rhode Islanders under the command of Artemas Ward, a veteran of the French and Indian War who commanded the Massachusetts army. And subsequently the Army of Observation was assigned to the right wing of the Massachusetts force at Roxbury overlooking the British redoubts on Boston Neck. Therefore, Greene's troops were not involved in the very bloody Battle of Breed's Hill (Bunker Hill) on June 17. The day after the battle, Greene wrote to Nicholas Cooke, the acting governor of Rhode Island, that the American soldiers had distinguished themselves, but that because of a "want of Powder they were after a great struggle forced to give way."[4]

On June 15, the Continental Congress selected forty-three-year-old George Washington of Virginia as commander in chief of the Continental Army. A week later the Congress authorized commissions for a number of other senior officers, including four major generals and eight brigadier generals. Nathanael Greene was appointed as one of the latter. Among the brigadier generals, Greene was the lowest ranking, but he accepted the position without complaint. At thirty-two he was the youngest general in the Continental Army. Responding to the actions of the Congress, the Rhode Island legislature on June 28 placed Greene under the commander in chief of the Continental Army, but only for the duration of that campaign.

When Washington arrived at Cambridge in early July, Greene wrote to Samuel Ward in the Continental Congress that the Virginian was "universally admird. Joy was visable on every countenance and it seemd as if the spirit of conquest breathed through the whole army. I hope we shall be taught to copy his example and to prefer the Love of Liberty in this time of publick danger to all the soft pleasures of domestic Life and support ourselves with manly fortitude amidst all the dangers and hardships that attend a state of war." But Greene also recognized that war could be a springboard from relative anonymity to historical immortality. "We are Soldiers," declared Greene, "who devote ourselves to arms not for the invasion of other Countries but for the defence of our own; not for the gratification of our own private Interest, but for the Publick security. Nevertheless they that assume this Character and possess a happy Genius accompanyed with a prudent conduct and fortune smiles on their endeavors, they have an Opportunity of traveling the shortest Road to the greatest heights of Ambition, and may the deserving obtain what their merit entitles them to."[5]

On July 22 Washington selected generals to command three divisions and six brigades. Greene was assigned to lead one of the latter. The army was comprised of three wings which defended the siege lines near Boston. General Ward commanded the right, or southern, wing, which was opposite Boston Neck. General Charles Lee was assigned the left wing, which extended from Charlestown peninsula to Cambridge. And Gen. Israel Putnam commanded the center wing, which defended the area from Cambridge to Roxbury. Located at Prospect Hill, Greene's brigade, which now also included four Massachusetts regiments, was one of two under Lee's command.

In the following months Washington made significant progress in organizing and staffing the Continental Army by often following British precedents and policies. Exceeding the 22,000 men the Continental Congress had authorized, by mid-October the army consisted of artillery, rifle, and some other separate companies, and thirty-eight New England infantry regiments, including three from Rhode Island. During this period, as Greene was involved in carrying out his many duties, including implementing discipline and organization, he wrote to Caty, who was pregnant with their first child, about the death of Augustus Mumford, first clerk of the Kentish Guards. He was killed when his head was blown off by a British cannonball while he was helping to fortify Plowed Hill. Greene asserted, "The fears and apprehensions for my safety, under your present debilitated state, must be a weight too great for you to support. We are all in the hands of the great Jehovah, to him let us look for protection. I trust that our controversy is a Righteous one, and altho many of our friends and rellatives may suffer an untimely fate, yet we must consider the evil Justified by the Righteousness of the dispute."[6]

In early September, as Caty spent an extended visit with her husband at Prospect Hill, Washington convened a council of war that consisted of the major generals and brigadier generals, including

Greene. The commander in chief wanted their views concerning the idea of an attack on the British at Boston and Roxbury. After a lengthy discussion, the council decided that it would not be expedient to initiate an attack at that time. A month later it again opposed the idea, although Greene asserted that an attack might be feasible if ten thousand soldiers could be landed at Boston. In the following months, Washington became even more impatient, as he sought an opportunity to strike at the British in Boston to raise American morale and to silence those who had criticized the army's inactivity. Therefore, in mid-January the council members unanimously supported an assault on Boston, if thirteen regiments of two-month militiamen arrived by February 1 and an adequate amount of weapons and gunpowder was procured.

On November 4, as recommended by Washington, the Continental Congress had sanctioned the reorganization of the army's infantry into twenty-six regiments. Each would consist of 640 privates and corporals, 32 sergeants, and 32 officers. Subsequently, on January 1, 1776, Washington announced in his general orders that the reorganization of the army was to commence in order to create a truly continental force. As a part of the reorganization, Rhode Island's three regiments would be reduced to two, which were to be the 9th and 11th Continental regiments.

But in early 1776, as these changes in the Continental Army were being implemented, Greene became quite ill. His relentless work schedule had taken a toll on his health, and in late January he developed jaundice. To his brother Jacob he asserted, "I am as yellow as saffron . . . and . . . I am so weak that I can scarcely walk across the room. . . . I am grievously mortified at my confinement, as this is a critical, and to appearance, will be an important period of the American War." Nevertheless, later in February Greene's spirits were raised when he received word that Caty had given birth to their first child, a son that they named George Washington Greene.[7]

In early February fifty-nine cannon had arrived at Cambridge. They had been brought from Fort Ticonderoga in an extraordinary feat of military engineering directed by Henry Knox. As a result, in mid-February Washington again proposed an all-out attack on Boston before the ice melted and prevented an assault across the Charles River.

The council of war, however, opposed Washington's plan because of insufficient troops and a significant shortage of gunpowder that prevented the use of artillery in support of an attack. Because of his illness, Greene was unable to attend the meeting, but it was known that he still did not support an attack because of the shortages faced by the Continental Army.

By early March, however, the generals supported a plan by Washington that could lead to an American attack on Boston. Having obtained a moderate stock of powder and called in the local militia to occupy fortifications, Washington placed cannon on Dorchester Heights on March 4. He hoped that the British would strike at the heights, which would allow Washington to send four thousand Continentals across the Charles River in a very daring attack on Boston. Six months earlier forty-six-year-old Gen. William Howe, who had been in the British army since age seventeen, had replaced General Gage as the commander in chief of British forces in North America. Howe now planned an assault on Dorchester Heights, despite his recognition that an assault on the American artillery would result in even more casualties than the Battle of Breed's Hill. A great storm, however, on the night of March 5–6 created huge waves that prevented any amphibious landings. As a result, Howe and Washington had to cancel their planned assaults. Moreover, the British commander in chief evacuated Boston on March 17, went to Canada to await reinforcements, and prepared to attack the Americans at a location where they seemed most vulnerable. Therefore, soon the attention of both sides would be focused on New York. And Greene, the neophyte general, would have an important role in shaping the American defense.

Escape (1776)

T HROUGHOUT THE Revolutionary War, British operations would be plagued by transportation, communication, supply,
and manpower problems. Indeed, though the British had a professional army and a large navy, practically every other advantage was on
the American side, including a more effective command system, the
use of interior lines, and the overall quality of its officer corps. Nevertheless, in June–July 1776 a British fleet of seventy-three ships under
the command of Adm. Richard Howe, Sir William's brother, carried
thirty-two thousand troops to New York Bay. In addition, Sir Guy
Carleton was preparing to lead 13,500 soldiers southward from Canada
down the Richelieu River–Lake Champlain route. This would be
Britain's largest military effort of the war.

Focusing their strategy on the middle colonies, the British plan
was to seize New York City with its superb harbor, control the Hudson
River, and then occupy all of the middle colonies with their supposedly large loyalist population, which would separate the more mili-
tant New England from the rest of the colonies. In piecemeal fashion
the revolutionary movement could then be crushed.

The day after the British evacuated Boston, Washington began
sending troops toward New York, since he believed that Howe probably

would move against the city. Washington and the Congress felt the defense of New York was of great importance because of its military significance and the effect its loss would have on the morale in other American cities. When Greene arrived on April 17, Washington placed him in command of the American forces on Long Island. Both recognized that the area was crucial to defend New York. The most extensive fortifications were built on the Heights of Guian in northwest Long Island, where Washington placed 5,800 troops, mostly militiamen.

During the following months, Greene wrote to Washington and John Adams, a prominent member of the Continental Congress, that the expansion of the army would require the fair treatment of the officers in terms of salaries and promotions; without this, many would probably leave the service. To Adams, Greene stated that the Congress should consult with Washington before making any promotions, and Greene declared that he would resign if the Congress promoted a junior officer over him. Driven by ambition and personal honor as much as duty, Greene felt he could serve only if the Congress dealt fairly with him.

Since September 1775, Greene had been outspoken regarding the issue of colonial independence. He initially asserted that he would be glad to continue the imperial connection if Britain's "tyrannical measures" which threatened political slavery were ended and American freedom preserved. But a month later he stated that military personnel "began heartily to wish a Declaration of Independence." When Greene heard in mid-December that the King called for military action to end the American rebelliousness, he wrote to his brother Jacob, "We are now driven to the necessity of making a declaration of independence. We can no longer preserve our freedom and continue the connection with [Britain]." And in early January 1776 he encouraged Samuel Ward in the Continental Congress to promote the idea of independence and thus allow America to "raise an Empire of Permanent Duration, supported upon the Grand Pillars of Truth, Freedom and Religion, encouraged by the smiles of Justice and defended by her own Patriotick Sons." Greene especially recognized that independence could lead to military assistance from France, which would make it much more difficult for the British to wage war against the Americans. Therefore, when news arrived in New York in early July that independence had been declared, Greene celebrated with the rest of the army.[1]

The war of liberation had begun. But it would not be a traditional conflict between nation-states regarding dynastic or economic concerns. Instead, this war of national self-determination was meant to protect "self-evident" natural rights by establishing a republican form of government under which sovereignty changed hands from the King in Parliament to the people. And this defense of individual liberty was dependent on civic virtue, which meant that citizens' participation in public affairs was essential to prevent the abuse of power in government and in society. The American War for Independence thus initiated a new era in Western warfare that would eventually affect all of the European empires.

When the British established a position on Staten Island in early July, Washington considered an attack, but Greene opposed the idea, partly because he worried about the size of the British force and the American army's lack of training. Like Washington, however, he also recognized the Continental Army's vulnerable position, as it was spread out on Manhattan Island and Long Island. Greene thus asserted that the Continental Army was involved in a "desperate [risky] game." Nevertheless, he believed that Americans behind barricades could defend their position.[2]

In July, however, typhoid, typhus, and smallpox incapacitated thousands of the American soldiers. Then on August 14, Greene, who recently had been promoted to major general, also fell ill, and two days later he became worse with a high fever. By the following afternoon his condition was critical. Greene was then turned over to the care of his brother Christopher, who was in New York on a business trip. Despite this care, he remained quite ill even two weeks later.

Greene's illness forced Washington, on August 24, to give his command to Israel Putnam, who sent four thousand soldiers to defend the roads leading to the Brooklyn fortifications, but failed to provide sufficient defense for the Jamaica Pass, where the British were concentrating their troops. Two days later General Howe launched his attack on Long Island. The British gave the Americans a sound drubbing and sent them fleeing, as the American force lost 1,400 men. Greene soon wrote, "I have not the vanity to think the event would have been otherwise had I been there." But no one knew the soldiers and the terrain on Long Island better than Greene, and he was a better tactician than Putnam. Greene probably would not have moved so many troops forward from the Brooklyn fortifications. And it seems unlikely that Greene would have failed to provide an adequate defense for the Jamaica Pass, which the British used for their breakthrough against the American force. Though Howe's twenty thousand professional troops posed a great threat to the much smaller and largely untrained

American force that included many militia, Greene's tactical skills might have prevented the debacle of August 26. Nevertheless, the Americans would still have faced entrapment on the island. Washington's dividing of the army to protect New York City had made that almost certain.[3]

But Howe did not press his advantage against the Americans behind fortifications on the western end of Long Island. Fearing another Breed's Hill, he preferred to starve them out. A great storm, however, on the night of August 29–30 prevented the British fleet from controlling the East River and allowed more than nine thousand Americans, under the cover of a dense fog, to escape across the river in a spectacular evacuation carried out largely by John Glover's and Israel Hutchinson's regiments of fishermen.

On September 5 Greene resumed some activities as his health began to return. He immediately wrote to Washington that New York City could no longer be defended since Long Island and Governor's Island were in British hands. Moreover, the British could now trap the Americans on Manhattan Island by controlling the East River and Hudson River and landing troops on the northernmost part of the island. In short, the Continental Army was in a very precarious situation. Therefore, Greene asserted that "a General and speedy Retreat is absolutely necessary and that the honnor and Interest of America requires it." The outcome of the revolution depended on saving the army. In addition, Greene advocated a scorched earth policy as a part of the retreat. He proposed the burning of New York City and its suburbs to eliminate the markets and housing that the British otherwise would use.[4]

Two days later Washington convened a council of war to discuss the exact issues that Greene had raised. A majority of Washington's staff advised holding the city at least temporarily, but Greene adamantly opposed the idea for the reasons he had stated in his letter to Washington. The commander in chief, however, accepted the majority opinion. Later, in private, Greene again expressed his opposition, and on September 11 Greene and six other officers broke army custom by sending a petition to Washington strongly requesting that he reconsider the decision to keep much of the Continental Army on Manhattan Island. Clearly Greene had been persuasive with some of the general officers after the September 7 meeting in order to reverse their views. The day after Washington received the petition, he held another council of war. Ten of the thirteen officers present, including Greene, voted to reconsider the decision to hold Manhattan Island. Thus, on September 14 Washington informed the Congress that he intended to evacuate New York City and retreat from the island. Greene's astute assessment of the situation would be crucial to the survival of the army.

Though Greene had been placed in charge of the "Centre Division" on September 1, he did not assume command until he had completely recovered in mid-September. Therefore, he was not actively involved in the evacuation of forces from New York City. As General Howe failed to move quickly, the British lost a golden opportunity to trap Washington's army on Manhattan Island. When the British finally attempted on September 15 to prevent the American escape, their limited effort failed.

On September 16, as the British occupied New York City, the retreating Continental Army became involved in a skirmish with the vanguard of the British force at Harlem Heights. The small battle, which eventually involved about two thousand men on each side, found the Americans forcing the British beyond Morningside Heights into a buckwheat field. When both sides sent reinforcements, Greene experienced his first combat up close. Along with Israel Putnam and Joseph Reed, he attempted to inspire the Americans by riding among them. As the British and Hessians began to run out of ammunition after two hours of fighting, they retreated with the Americans in pursuit. But with British reserves nearby, Washington ended the attack since he did not want the fighting to turn into a full-fledged battle. Nevertheless, the skirmish had clearly been a boost to the American morale.

The next day, Washington ordered Greene to organize the defense of New Jersey. As the days passed without another British attack, the Rhode Islander asserted that it seemed strange Howe would wait so long after taking New York to continue the campaign. But a month after the Battle of Harlem Heights, Howe again tried to encircle the American army by landing four thousand soldiers at Throg's Neck (variously called Frog's Neck or Frog's Point), which was either a peninsula or island, depending on the tides and water drainage. Howe had thus outflanked the Continental Army at Harlem Heights, which compelled Washington to withdraw his force to White Plains.

In early October, charged with the defense of Fort Washington, which was located on steep cliffs on the Manhattan side of the Hudson River, Greene had sent another regiment to shore up its defenses. He argued that the fort could be held indefinitely if it were properly defended. And maintaining the fort would force Howe to keep a significant part of his force on Manhattan Island. Washington, though doubtful of the feasibility of defending the fort, deferred to the Rhode Islander's judgment. Greene, however, was overlooking a crucial fact. The fort had no water supply, and thus a siege could within days bring disaster to the more than 2,900 Americans inside.

In early November, British ships sailed up the Hudson River, as the vessels were not stopped by American cannon in Fort Washington or obstructions in the river. Nevertheless, Greene was convinced of the fort's strategic importance, and he remained confident that it could be defended. He probably hoped that a British attack on the fortress, like Breed's Hill earlier in the war, would result in numerous enemy casualties. But on November 16 Howe sent ten thousand soldiers against the American garrison. And when he wheeled his artillery into place, the American commander, Col. Robert Magaw, agreed to surrender.

The fall of Fort Washington shocked and dismayed Greene. To Henry Knox he wrote, "I feel mad, vexed, sick, and sorry." He blamed the officers and soldiers for not attempting to properly defend the fort. Clearly, however, Greene had misevaluated the quality of the troops and their leaders. But, more importantly, he failed to see that the lack of a water supply would have meant eventual disaster for even the best of soldiers. In short, Greene's decision to defend Fort Washington was the worst mistake he made during the war.[5]

In the days following the surrender of the fort, Washington and other officers began to have doubts about Greene's judgment. But he remained in command of Fort Lee, on the west side of the Hudson River opposite Fort Washington. Greene, like Washington, believed they still had time to cannibalize the fort of all needed supplies before abandoning it. On November 20, however, Greene was awakened by a report that approximately five thousand British soldiers under Gen. Lord Charles Cornwallis had landed at a seldom-used landing about six miles above Fort Lee and were rapidly advancing toward the fortress. Greene quickly led his men in an evacuation of the fort, thus barely averting another disaster for the Continental Army. Nevertheless, the losses at Fort Lee and especially Fort Washington were enormous. Besides the 2,900 troops who had been captured, the Americans lost nearly eight thousand cannon shot, four thousand cannon shells, twenty-eight hundred muskets, and four hundred thousand cartridges.

Because of supply shortages, however, Cornwallis did not begin to leave Fort Lee until November 29. A week later he united with the force under General Howe, who now envisioned possibly destroying Washington's army and then capturing the Continental Congress in Philadelphia. As Washington moved the Continental Army's supplies across the Delaware River into Pennsylvania, he sent a brigade under Greene to Princeton to slow the British advance. But on December 7, when his force was faced with the possibility of being outflanked, Greene ordered the brigade to withdraw. The next day Washington led his troops, which had dwindled to approximately 3,400 because of expiring enlistments and desertions, across the Delaware River, just ahead of the vanguard of the British army. Since the Americans had taken or destroyed all the boats in the area, Howe's pursuit of the Continental Army ended at the Delaware. Even so, Washington recognized the enormous danger the Continental Army still faced. On December 18, he wrote to his brother that if the Continental Army was not enlarged, "I think the game will be pretty well up."[6]

The situation was undeniably bleak. To John Hancock, the president of the Continental Congress, Greene declared, "Altho I am far from thinking the American Cause desperate, yet I conceive it to be in a critical situation." These were, as Tom Paine wrote in one of the most famous statements of the war, "times that try men's souls. The summer soldier and the sunshine patriot will, in this crisis, shrink from the service of his country." Indeed, an increase in the size of Washington's army was crucial. Just days before Christmas 2,600 soldiers under Generals John Sullivan and Horatio Gates arrived at the American camp, and Philadelphia Associators came to the support of the Continental Army. Most importantly, the British had now gone into winter encampment and the Continental Army remained intact. The great British offensive of 1776 had failed to end the revolution. In fact, General Howe had missed the best opportunity the British would have during the war to destroy Washington's army. And as long as the Continental Army remained in existence, in all likelihood the revolution would go on.[7]

Rebirth (1776–77)

By CHRISTMAS Washington had approximately six thousand soldiers who could be used against the British. Enlistments, however, for many of the troops would expire at the end of December. According to Greene, the situation in the Continental Army was critical because of the lack of new recruits, the inflation of the Continental currency, the insufficient number of cannon, discontentment among officers over the issue of promotions, and the failure of the people to provide supplies for the army. Regarding the lack of popular support, Greene asserted to John Hancock, "The Virtue of the People at such an Hour is not [to] be trusted." To better deal with these problems, Greene advocated giving extraordinary powers to Washington. Though he normally would oppose the extension of military authority in this fashion, he believed the current crisis made such action "absolutely necessary." To protect the revolution, its leaders would have to go beyond republicanism's fear of military authority. A week later Congress passed a resolution that gave Washington a great increase in powers for six months, as outlined in Greene's letter.[1]

At the time that he wrote to Hancock, Greene knew that Washington was planning an action against the enemy outposts in New Jersey in order to build up American morale and to encourage recruitment in the spring. At a meeting on Christmas Eve, Washington, Greene, and several other officers worked out the details of a surprise attack on the Hessian outpost at Trenton. At dusk on Christmas day, Washington led 2,400 troops from Greene's and Sullivan's divisions across the ice-filled Delaware River during a snow and sleet storm. They arrived at 3:00 a.m. about nine miles above Trenton. They did not begin their march toward the town until nearly 4:00; the operation was approximately four hours behind schedule. Halfway to the town, Washington sent the two divisions down different roads toward the Hessian outpost. Greene had the most difficult task, since he was to lead his division uphill along the Upper Ferry Road away from the Delaware River, which would bring the force to the Pennington Road and into the northern side of Trenton. Meanwhile, Sullivan's division was to continue along River Road and thus enter the southern side of the town.

But at dawn, as the American forces converged on Trenton, the sleet turned into a blinding snowstorm. Sullivan informed Washington that the snow was wetting the gunpowder in many of the muskets so that they could not be fired. "What is to be done?" asked Sullivan. Gen. Arthur St. Clair asserted, "You have nothing for it but to push on and charge." Washington concurred. "Advance and charge," he stated, despite the fact that no more than 20 percent of the soldiers had bayonets. The commander in chief then rode among the troops urging them to pick up the pace. Greene's troops, running in order through the snow, now entered the northern part of the town. "I never could conceive," Col. Clement Biddle later stated, "that one spirit should so universally animate both officers and men to rush forward into action." They quickly occupied the high ground, as they viewed all of Trenton below them. After the Americans swept over the enemy outposts, Washington had Knox's cannon blast the Hessians. Then Continental riflemen took deadly aim against the Germans. Within ninety minutes Washington's force, which did not suffer a single fatality, had taken more than nine hundred prisoners. Greene and Knox advocated pushing on against the other outposts south of Trenton, but Washington wisely retreated back across the Delaware River. After the victory, Greene wrote to Caty: "This is an important period to America, big with great events. God only knows what will be the issue of this

Campaign, but everything wears a much better prospect than they have for some weeks past." Indeed, Trenton provided a major psychological boost for the Continental Army.[2]

Buoyed up by the success at Trenton, Washington decided to strike again, and he convinced at least half of his veterans to stay for another six weeks after their enlistments ended at the end of the year. On December 30 he again led a part of his army across the Delaware River to Trenton, which the enemy had not reoccupied. From there the commander in chief wanted to move against the British outpost at Princeton. But Washington had miscalculated the British response to the fall of Trenton, and this almost led to the destruction of the Continental Army. General Cornwallis, an aggressive and very able officer, was rushing six thousand British troops toward Trenton. Greene's division, however, moved forward to slow their advance. A member of his division later wrote that the Rhode Islander encouraged his men by shouting "Push on boys! Push on!" Since the British did not arrive near Trenton until nightfall, Cornwallis decided to wait until the next day to attack the Americans. Thus, the delaying tactics of Greene's division may have saved the Continental Army.[3]

Caught between Trenton and the Delaware River by the arrival of Cornwallis's force, Washington conferred with Greene and other generals, and then decided on a very risky nighttime march along a back road toward the British outpost at Princeton. As the American campfires burned, Washington's army made its escape. But at sunrise the vanguard of the American force ran into two British regiments that were leaving Princeton to join Cornwallis. As the Americans began to fall back, Washington, Greene, and other officers rushed to the front to rally the troops, who soon overwhelmed the enemy. Led by Greene, some of the Continentals pursued the British toward Kingston before going with the rest of the American army to the hills near Morristown, where a camp had been established. As the Americans prepared to settle into their winter encampment, Greene and the rest of the army could savor the second small victory that further boosted American morale. And in three months Greene had the additional pleasure of hearing that Caty had given birth to their second child, a daughter, whom they named Martha Washington Greene. For months, however, Greene would remain worried by reports that his wife was weak and sick.

Howe decided to withdraw British forces from New Jersey, except at New Brunswick and Amboy. In fact, throughout the war, the British would find it very difficult to control territory beyond the coastal towns. Their efforts at pacification were partly undermined by British plundering and loyalist recriminations—including rapes—against those who supported the rebel cause.

By this point, Greene had regained Washington's confidence in his leadership. This soon led Washington to use a plan proposed by Greene for spreading out a Continental division in a series of posts between Morristown and the British positions. These posts would prevent the British from launching a surprise attack on the Continental Army.

But the number of soldiers in the American force continued to decline because of the end of terms of enlistment and desertion, including many deserters to the British ranks. The desertion problem became so great that Washington commented he would have to use half the American army to bring back the other half. And to make matters worse, smallpox began spreading among the ranks. To control the situation, Washington ordered the inoculation of the entire army.

In mid-March, further demonstrating his renewed confidence in Greene, Washington ordered him to Philadelphia to discuss various important matters with Congress, including its failure to allow the appointment of three lieutenant generals. The Rhode Islander was one of those denied this promotion. In addition, Greene promoted, and the Congress eventually adopted, his recommendation that it give medals of valor to officers who had distinguished themselves in combat. He declared that this would be an inexpensive way to promote morale and to increase the bonds between Congress and the army. After meeting with the Congress, Greene also surveyed the city and informed Washington that he did not believe it could be successfully defended because there were so many approaches to it.

By 1777 the *rage militaire* that had swept America during the war's first year had ended. Therefore, in the spring, the Congress recommended a draft to the states, although this was at odds with the republican concept of citizen-soldiers voluntarily coming to the defense of liberty. By this means hundreds of draftees, or those paid to substitute for draftees, became regulars in the Continental Army. But the Congress also raised new recruits by authorizing a bounty of twenty dollars plus one hundred acres for serving until the end of the war or a ten dollar bounty for three years' service. As a result, the newest Continentals were mostly from the poor and dependent classes, which had grown substantially, especially in the urban areas, in the twenty years before the Revolutionary War. Thus, ironically, the British offensive of 1776 and the subsequent collapse of patriotic enthusiasm for enlisting in the Continental Army had pushed the Congress into hiring a military force to defend the cause of republicanism, despite its traditional warnings about the dangers posed to liberty by standing armies.

By late May, as several thousand soldiers arrived at Morristown, Washington had about 7,360 effective troops, and he moved the Continental force to Middlebrook, about twenty miles south of Morristown. Howe, having assembled an army of eighteen thousand soldiers, hoped to draw Washington into a battle on the plains near Amboy. Despite some skirmishing, Washington refused to be pulled into a pitched battle. Then, at the end of June, Howe suddenly took his army to Staten Island. He had concluded that the capture of Philadelphia, where the Continental Congress met, would be crucial for ending the revolution.

Greene, however, believed Howe would be taking his army northward to upstate New York to join Gen. John Burgoyne, who in June initiated an invasion southward from Canada with an army of seven thousand troops to seize control of the upper part of the Hudson River valley. Therefore, under Washington's orders, Greene headed toward Beverwyck to direct efforts at collecting supplies for American forces sent to the Highlands. But also at Beverwyck Greene would be reunited with Caty after a year's separation. She would stay for a year in New Jersey. During this time, the Greene's two children, George and Martha, stayed with Greene's brothers, Jacob and Christopher.

Within days of Greene's arrival at Beverwyck, however, word arrived that the British had captured Fort Ticonderoga. Greene believed that Washington wanted him to replace Gen. Philip Schuyler as the commander of the Continental forces in the Northern Department, but Greene noted to Caty that he would decline the position if Washington gave him a choice. In the end, the commander in chief did not submit Greene's name to Congress for the command of the Northern

Army. Although Washington would have been reluctant to part with one of his most trusted advisors, he probably did not advise Congress to appoint Greene because he knew that the Rhode Islander had alienated most of the national legislature with his letters chastising Congress for appointing Phillippe de Coudray, a stuffy Frenchman who allegedly had significant experience with artillery, as a major general in the Continental Army. That appointment had given de Coudray rank above a number of long-serving generals. As Washington decided against recommending Greene, a group of New England delegates asked the commander in chief to endorse Gen. Horatio Gates for the position. But Washington did not favor Gates, and therefore he recommended no one. Congress, however, soon selected Gates to be supreme commander of the entire Northern Department.

On August 25, Howe's army of 12,500 troops arrived at the head of the Chesapeake Bay, about fifty-five miles from Philadelphia, and began its march toward the capital of the young American republic. Congress relocated from Philadelphia to Lancaster and then York. And Washington led his army of twelve thousand soldiers to Chadd's Ford on the east side of Brandywine Creek to block the British march on the City of Brotherly Love. The Brandywine was the final natural barrier on the road to Philadelphia. Without bridges or boats, the only viable places to cross Brandywine Creek were the shallow fords. Washington therefore would concentrate his troops at these locations to counter Howe's advance on Philadelphia. For the first time since the Battle of Long Island a year earlier, Washington's and Howe's forces would meet in what would turn out to be one of the war's largest battles.

Washington placed most of his cavalry and some militia and Continental brigades on the west side of the ford. But most of the army remained on the east side of the Brandywine, including Greene's division as a crucial reserve force for the American position. On September 11, a hot and humid day, Howe divided his army into two columns. Baron Wilhelm von Knyphausen led approximately five thousand troops to Chadd's Ford. Meanwhile, Howe, using a swift, wide envelopment tactic that had worked at the Battle of Long Island, led the rest of the army across the Brandywine about six miles north of Chadd's Ford in an attempt to outflank Washington's right wing. When

Washington and Greene received reports that Howe had divided his army, they felt he had committed a great blunder. Confident that the forces on the right flank of the American position could hold off Howe's advance, Washington and Greene decided that a movement by the American army across the Brandywine could shatter Knyphausen's force. This order, however, was countermanded when a militia officer reported that there was no sign of the British flanking force on the east side of the Brandywine. Washington now felt that Howe might have doubled back with his troops to reinforce Knyphausen and thereby draw the Americans into a trap on the west side of the creek. Actually, Howe's force had crossed the Brandywine, and thus poor intelligence reports prevented the Americans from perhaps inflicting a significant setback on the British army. Instead, the Americans were left unprepared for Howe's attack.

Finally realizing that Howe had led a force to the east side of the Brandywine, Washington ordered Greene to take one brigade of his division as quickly as possible to bolster the Continental Army's right flank against Howe's attack. If the American wing could not be stabilized, the Rhode Islander's force needed to cover the army's retreat. Greene's brigade, led by Gen. George Weedon, reached the scene of the fighting near Plowed Hill at about 6:00 p.m. after marching four miles in forty-five minutes. Outnumbered more than two-to-one, the American right wing faced a situation that was becoming desperate. Greene later wrote, "When I came upon the ground I found the whole of the troops routed and retreating precipitately, and in the most broken and confused manner." Greene's brigade could not restore the American position; instead, they could only provide a disciplined retreat as they fell back from position to position.[4]

Meanwhile, Knyphausen's force crossed the Brandywine under the cover of artillery to strike at the center of the American line. For two and a half hours, until the beginning of darkness around 7:00 p.m., the Americans fell back with a dogged defense. Eventually the retreating center line and right wing converged, and Greene's division held off the Hessians and British in twilight fighting. Indeed, Greene's division had clearly saved the Continental Army. Nevertheless, the retreating American force was largely unorganized as soldiers stumbled along in the dark on the road to Chester. Greene, however, was able to keep his division together, and Washington and he were able to re-store order to the Continental ranks near Chester. The Americans had lost approximately 200 killed, 500 wounded, and 400 captured, while the British lost 90 killed and 448 wounded. But Washington could scrape up replacements for his losses, and Howe could not. Most importantly, Washington had avoided a disastrous defeat and the army survived to fight another day.

Washington and Greene led the Continental Army to Germantown and then to a location near Warren's Tavern to reorganize and to resupply. Greene wrote to Caty, "Our troops are in good health and high Spirits and wish for action again." When Howe ordered Cornwallis and Knyphausen to advance in widely separated columns toward the Americans, Greene felt this offered an extraordinary opportunity to attack the enemy.

But on September 16, as Washington prepared his force for battle, a major part of the army remained without supplies because of confusion by some of the commissaries. After spending hours obtaining supplies, both armies were caught in a powerful rainstorm that prevented any attack. Therefore, what could have been a major battle of the war turned into what became known as "The Battle of the Clouds."[5]

The following day Washington was informed that the shortage of ammunition was worse than previously reported, and he decided to withdraw the army to a more secure location until ammunition could be acquired. Greene soon found a site on the side of a range of mountains near Warwick, where the army would be secure from attack but still in a position to harass Howe's army. But Washington, without waiting for Greene's return, called a council of war and accepted its recommendation to move the army to a location east of the Schuylkill River between Philadelphia and the British, though a detachment of troops under Gen. Anthony Wayne would be kept on the other side of the river near Paoli Tavern as a rear guard. Washington, however, would soon regret ignoring Greene's proposal for an encampment in the mountains. In a nighttime attack on September 21, while using only bayonets, three British regiments overran Wayne's camp. Two hundred Americans were killed in the "Paoli Massacre."

Howe subsequently outmaneuvered Washington, and on September 25 he encamped most of his army near Germantown, while five miles away General Cornwallis occupied Philadelphia with grenadiers and dragoons. Nevertheless, Washington soon had eleven thousand troops in the American army, including eight thousand Continentals. Therefore, Greene felt the Americans should attack when an opportunity presented itself. Indeed, he believed a surprise attack would bring a major victory to the Americans. When intelligence reports indicated that Howe had sent large detachments from Germantown to obtain supplies and to attack the American fort at Billingsport, New Jersey, Greene strongly supported Washington's decision to strike at Howe's force, which now totaled approximately nine thousand soldiers.

On October 3, at Centre Point, Washington finalized his plan of attack, and at 7:00 p.m. the American troops began the fifteen-mile march to Germantown. Although much like the strike against Trenton, this plan was even more daring because the enemy was the main British army. Washington intended to use a pincer movement of four columns down the four roads to Germantown to trap and attack the British with the Schuykill River at their back. The principal attack was to be led by three large divisions under Greene on the left center and three smaller divisions led by Sullivan on the right center. The columns on the extreme left and right were comprised mainly of militia.

But traveling in darkness over unfamiliar roads, the American army did not cover the distance that Washington anticipated. At dawn, as a heavy fog moved into the area, Sullivan's divisions, the closest to Germantown, were still behind schedule. Nevertheless, they pushed back and then routed the British light pickets. Soon, however, a full British regiment reinforced the small number of defenders. As they were surrounded by the American advance, about 120 of the British barricaded themselves in a large stone house, owned by Justice Benjamin Chew, that was halfway between the British outposts and their main camp. From this position British marksmen began to pick off American soldiers. General Knox, head of the American artillery, who drew on classical military theory, now asserted that an army could not have an enemy fortress at its rear. During the next hour, the Americans suffered about one hundred casualties as they made futile attempts to bombard and storm the house. Moreover, this slowed down the American advance and led General Wayne, whom Greene later described as "the Modern hero" due to his spirited romanticism, to send his division back toward the house since he thought Sullivan's force was in trouble.[6]

During the first thirty minutes of the battle, Greene's divisions were nowhere in sight since his guide had lost his way and the troops were several miles from the intended location. Some individuals would later blame Greene for the lateness of his division, but Washington did not accept this, and Greene would assert that the accusation was "as infamous a falsehood as ever was reported." He further stated regarding Germantown, "I think if ever I merited anything it was for my exertions on that day." Always concerned about how "all future generations" would judge his performance, the Rhode Islander declared, "I trust history will do justice to the reputations of individuals."[7]

Once his force arrived at Limekiln Road, Greene took his division to the left of the road, and ordered Gen. Adam Stephen's division to the right of Limekiln and Gen. Alexander McDougall's to the far left. But the combination of fog, woods, marshes, and fence lines hampered their advance. Whereas McDougall's division never got into the fighting, Stephen's division would veer to the right, as it responded to the firing at the Chew House, and in the heavy fog it became involved in an exchange of volleys with Wayne's division on Sullivan's left. Meanwhile, Greene led his division into increasingly intense fighting. Col. George Mathews's Ninth Virginia Regiment went so far ahead of the rest of the division that it was surrounded, and the British captured four hundred troops. Since Sullivan's division, which was running out of ammunition, and Wayne's division were now making a hasty retreat, the British under Gen. James Grant focused their effort against Greene's division, and Greene lost more soldiers before he was able to withdraw the rest of his men. With Wayne's division, Greene's force provided cover for the fleeing American troops. By this point, Cornwallis had arrived from Philadelphia with three battalions, and Washington recognized that the American force was experiencing a piecemeal retreat that the officers could not stop. Therefore, he ordered a general retreat that eventually took the exhausted army back to its former camp at Pennypacker's Mill.

Washington's intricate plan of attack had failed, and the Battle of Germantown became a British victory. Washington had lost about 1,100 men and Howe had suffered about half that many. But Washington again was able to replace his losses and Howe could not. Despite the defeat at Germantown, the American officers and soldiers remained optimistic. Greene believed that the battle demonstrated the Continental Army's ability to hold its own against the British, if fortune was fair in dealing with both armies.

Gen. Adam Stephen was accused of "unofficerlike behaviour" for not rallying his troops during the retreat from Germantown and for being frequently intoxicated during his service in the Continental Army. In fact, he had been found lying in a fence corner very intoxicated during the retreat. In this case, however, the consuming of alcohol may have been an effort to counter the effects of combat fatigue. Nevertheless, Greene headed the court of enquiry, which accumulated evidence in support of the charges. Subsequently Stephen was court-martialed, found guilty, and dismissed from the service.

Meanwhile, General Burgoyne's invasion from Canada, which began in June 1777, had floundered in upstate New York. His troops became bogged down in the wilderness and received no assistance from Howe. Militia and Continental forces encircled Burgoyne's army and eventually forced its capitulation at the village of Saratoga on October 17, 1777. News of the surrender electrified the American public. Greene, despite undoubtedly having some sense of envy, took pride in the American victory, and he recognized that this would lead to reinforcements being sent from the Northern Army to the main Continental force, which he hoped "will enable . . . [us] to give the enemy a decisive blow." More importantly, the surrender of Burgoyne's army would be a significant factor in persuading the French to form a military alliance with the United States in early 1778, making the revolutionary conflict in America into a world war with substantial benefits for the American cause.[8]

To maintain control of Philadelphia, the British needed to control the Delaware River in order to ensure a constant flow of supplies. But *chevaux-de-frise*, rock-filled wooden frames on which sharpened timbers were set at an angle to rip the hull of a vessel, had been placed in the river, and the Americans controlled Fort Mercer on the New Jersey side and Fort Mifflin on the Pennsylvania side. Greene, who had spent considerable time analyzing the issue of defending the Delaware River, advocated reinforcing Fort Mercer. Remembering criticisms over the loss of Fort Washington, Greene placed four hundred Rhode Islanders in the fort, including a regiment commanded by Christopher Greene, Nathanael's third cousin. They subsequently staved off an attack by two thousand Hessians, who suffered four hundred casualties. It was the largest percentage of casualties suffered by the enemy since Breed's Hill. And Nathanael Greene was elated when he heard the news of the successful defense.

Unable to knock out Fort Mercer, Howe concentrated on Fort Mifflin. Beginning on November 10, the British bombarded the fort for five days. Washington eventually gave Greene permission to reinforce the fort, but before it could be done the British brought warships so near the fort that hand grenades could be thrown inside. More importantly, the ships' cannon blasted the fort. As Pvt. Joseph Plumb Martin stated: "the enemy's shot ate us up." On November 15 the Americans abandoned the fort after setting it on fire. Washington then ordered Greene to reinforce Fort Mercer with a division, but before it arrived, word reached Greene that the defenders had evacuated the fort.[9]

As Greene prepared to leave New Jersey, Washington encouraged him to attack the British force under General Cornwallis that had been sent there to capture Fort Mercer. Greene recognized that Washington was facing increasing criticism for supposedly using only Fabian tactics, but Greene asserted to Washington, "The Cause is too important to be trifled with to shew our Courage, and your Character too deeply interested to sport away upon unmilitary Principles." Nevertheless, if Washington still wanted an attack, Greene stated that he would "run any Risque or engage under any Disadvantages." At the same time, Greene staunchly opposed an attack on Philadelphia. He asserted that it would be "a hassardous attempt and will terminate to the injury of the Continent and disgrace of the army." Immediately after receiving Greene's letter, Washington instructed him to bring his division back to Pennsylvania to protect the Continental Army against a possible attack by the main British force. General Howe did maneuver his army for several days, but Greene had returned by this time and the Continental Army held a very strong defensive position near White Marsh. Therefore, Howe returned to Philadelphia and the British army settled down for the winter.[10]

Washington soon led his army into winter encampment at Valley Forge, about eighteen miles from Philadelphia. The New Jersey and Pennsylvania campaigns of 1776–77 had come to an end. The British controlled the capital city of the United States, but that had not moved them an inch closer to ending the revolution. Indeed, despite the setbacks of the previous year, the Continental Army had demonstrated its resiliency. American victories at Trenton and Princeton and aggressiveness at Germantown, though overshadowed by the surrender of Burgoyne's army at Saratoga, had substantially bolstered the American morale. Greene, who had been at the center of much of the action, could take great satisfaction in the development of the army. From near disaster in the New York campaign in 1776, the Continental Army had been, in a sense, reborn, and during the upcoming winter at Valley Forge, it would be transformed into a truly professional military force.

Transformation (1777–80)

T HE CONTINENTAL army remained encamped at Valley Forge, Pennsylvania, from December 1777 to June 1778. About twelve men were housed in each log hut, while the officers found lodging in private homes. Valley Forge, however, was not in a prosperous farming area, and the local population included many loyalists who were unwilling to aid the army. Therefore, the Continentals had to bring in supplies over a great distance using poor roads. Moreover, runaway inflation had undermined the Continental currency, and inefficiency in the Quartermaster and Commissary Departments substantially contributed to the shortage of supplies. In February 1778 Washington reported that at least four thousand men were unfit for any kind of duty. During the Continental Army's encampment at Valley Forge, approximately 2,500 soldiers died from diseases, malnutrition, and exposure. In addition, scores of officers resigned their commissions, and the desertion rate continued to rise.

On February 8–9 a major snowstorm prevented any supplies from reaching the army. This made an already bad situation even worse, as the army came close to starvation. Washington quickly ordered Greene, Wayne, and Henry "Light-Horse Harry" Lee to organize foraging parties to scour Pennsylvania, Delaware, and New Jersey for supplies.

Mostly because of Greene's organizational skills, the American foragers found substantial amounts of hay and obtained a large number of animals. The Americans gave receipts for the livestock and other supplies, though Greene decreed that those who tried to hide their animals would receive no receipts. Greene also personally led the foraging on the islands in the Delaware River, where a significant number of horses was found. He also ordered the burning of whatever hay could not be taken to Valley Forge, to prevent the surplus from falling into British hands. This action may have alienated farmers in these areas, but Greene believed many were already loyalists.

As the winter wore on, criticism of Washington began to increase substantially both in and out of Congress. Some of the critics, especially outside of Congress, began to suggest that Gen. Horatio Gates, considered by many the hero of Saratoga, could provide better leadership for the Continental Army. As Benjamin Rush, a Philadelphia physician and former surgeon general of the army, asserted, "Look at both, the one [Gates] on the pinnacle of military glory—the other [Washington] out-generaled and twice beaten." Greene became convinced that Thomas Mifflin and Gates, whom he referred to as "a mere child of fortune," were behind the effort to replace Washington.[1]

Washington had tried to avoid commenting on the criticisms. But then he received word of critical comments about his army allegedly made to General Gates by Gen. Thomas Conway, an Irishman who had served in the French army. Washington wrote a brief, harsh note to Conway, who denied using the words Washington had cited, and Conway offered to show the commander in chief the original letter. Subsequently, however, Congress appointed Mifflin and Gates to the Board of War, which had been created in June 1776 to give Congress more control over the military. The Congress also now appointed Conway inspector general of the army, after promoting him to major general. To Washington and Greene this series of events, later called the Conway Cabal, was evidence of a conspiracy to replace Washington. Actually there was no plan to get rid of Washington; but battlefield losses, the grueling winter encampment, and ongoing disputes with Congress concerning promotions and other issues had made the commander in chief, Greene, and several fellow generals excessively sensitive.

Nevertheless, there were tensions between the Board of War and

Washington. These increased in early 1778 when the Board of War proposed a diversionary invasion of Canada. Greene opposed the plan, which he felt could achieve little and would drain needed supplies away from Washington's army. Moreover, Greene believed the plan had been developed by the board to give Conway an independent command. Indeed, Gates and Mifflin argued that Conway's service in the French army gave him the needed background for trying to win over French support in Canada. But Washington countered this by declaring that the Marquis de Lafayette would be the logical choice to lead the expedition. After Congress appointed Lafayette, however, the Marquis concluded that there were insufficient supplies and men for an invasion. Therefore, in the end, Greene's original assessment of the impracticality of the plan was validated. Soon afterward, when Conway again threatened to resign his commission, Congress accepted the offer, and Washington finally was rid of his antagonistic subordinate.

In February the Continental Congress began discussions to appoint a new quartermaster general. As one of several supply departments within the army, the Quartermaster Department purchased and distributed supplies other than food, clothing, medical goods, and arms and ammunition. It also moved and encamped the army. But its most vital function was the transporting of all supplies. Since the British blockade had ended most coastal trade, the Continental Army was forced to move most of its supplies using inadequate means of transportation over inadequate roads.

The Continental Congress soon offered the position to Greene. But he was very reluctant to give up the opportunity to lead men in battle and thus gain "honor and laurels." Greene asserted to Alexander McDougall, "All of you will be immortallising your selves in the golden pages of History, while I am confined to a series of drudgery to pave the way for it." Nevertheless, he certainly recognized that he could gain financially from the position since he and his two assistants would equally divide a one percent commission on all purchases. But it was primarily his sense of patriotism that compelled him to accept the position, as he wanted to avoid undermining the army, to aid Washington who had been forced to do the work up to that point, and to promote the public good.[2]

As quartermaster general, Greene supervised hundreds of men, and eventually the Quartermaster Department engaged more than three thousand people at a cost of more than four hundred thousand dollars per month. Despite his lack of enthusiasm for the position, Greene's commission on purchases brought him a significant amount of money, which he had friends invest for him in real estate, privateering, shipping, and manufacturing. Since he purchased some supplies from Jacob Greene and Company, which he still partly owned, he was guilty of nepotism. There is no evidence that the company sold supplies above the going rate. Nevertheless, the transactions exposed Greene to assertions that he was involved in some type of impropriety. Greene, however, never believed that any of his actions as quartermaster general were dishonorable.

Several months after becoming quartermaster general, Greene wrote to Thomas McKean, who was the chief justice of Pennsylvania, requesting that he postpone the appearance in court of Robert Lettis Hooper Jr., who was the deputy quartermaster general. Hooper had granted safe-conduct passes to individuals who wanted to visit members of the British army, which had been occupying Philadelphia. This action was eventually reported by the Pennsylvania Supreme Executive Council to the Continental Board of War. As Congress considered the matter, Hooper threatened Jacob Arndt, who had informed the Pennsylvania Supreme Executive Council of Hooper's actions, and then Hooper threatened the Council itself. Greene asserted that he did not wish to interfere with the court's proceedings, but that he "could not without great Necessity consent to . . . [Hooper] being absent as there is no other Person that can give the Necessary Aid [to the army] upon this Occasion." He assured McKean that he would guarantee Hooper's appearance in court in the near future. In asserting the civil government's supremacy over the military, McKean heatedly replied that "I shall not ask *your consent* nor that of any other person in or out of the army" for having Hooper appear in court as scheduled. Thus Greene's initial dealings with state officials did not go well. And his subsequent dealings with them during the rest of his tenure as quartermaster general would go no better.[3]

Despite serving as quartermaster general, Greene remained a principal military advisor to Washington. Indeed, in a sense, Greene's value to the commander in chief now doubled since he was serving as both an advisor and an administrator. As an advisor, he recognized that during the winter at Valley Forge, the Continental Army had been transformed into a more disciplined fighting force, thanks in part to the drill tactics and training practices used by Friedrich von Steuben, a pretended baron who had served as a captain in the Prussian army. On June 18, the day after Washington held a council of war, Greene correctly speculated that Gen. Henry Clinton, a capable strategist and tactician who had replaced Howe as commander of British forces in May, would lead the British army of ten thousand troops across New Jersey back to New York. Greene advised that any decision for a particular general attack on the British would have to depend on the circumstances of such a move. But Greene concluded that "I would not risque a General action if it can well be avoided, unless I had some great advantage from the make of the ground or the manner of attack. Neither would I make any attack at all if it should appear at the time to be against our interest." But six days later, following another council of war, Greene asserted, "I think we can make a very serious impression without any great risque, and if it should amount to a general action I think the chance is greatly in our favor. However I think we can make a partial attack without suffering them to bring us to a general action."[4]

In command of more than 10,500 soldiers, Washington now decided to seek an action against the rear and left flank of the British army stretched out on the roads back to New York. In particular, he decided to send 1,500 troops to combine with the Continentals and militia already near the British. Gen. Charles Lee, who had been released as a prisoner of war in May, turned down command of the small attack force because he considered it inappropriate for someone of his rank. Since Lee had opposed an attack on Clinton's army and held an openly pessimistic view of the Continentals' ability to fight the British, Washington probably was not disappointed with Lee's decision. The commander in chief instead appointed twenty-year-old Lafayette, despite his inexperience as a field commander, to lead the attack. However, when Washington increased the size of the attacking force, Lee decided that he wanted to assume the command, which he did on June 27. Washington then ordered Lee to plan an attack for the next morning against the enemy's rearguard near Monmouth Courthouse.

On the twenty-eighth, Lee, with no good knowledge of the terrain or of British strength—which was about six thousand soldiers—led the American vanguard over three ravines. Because the terrain hindered communications, prevented the quick arrival of reinforcements, and posed the danger of being trapped against a ravine, Lee ordered his troops to retreat after some initial skirmishing with the British rearguard. But as Lee reached the last ravine, Washington admonished him for falling back and established a line of battle just to the west. The British attacked several times at different locations along the line, but the Americans held their ground, firing numerous volleys into the advancing enemy line. The temperature by this time had reached nearly one hundred degrees Fahrenheit and the soldiers, in wool uniforms and carrying heavy packs, suffered greatly. Many troops would succumb to heat stroke. In addition, for two hours the soldiers witnessed a thunderous artillery exchange which was the heaviest cannonade of the war. During this exchange, Mary Ludwig Hays, later known as Molly Pitcher, achieved fame for supposedly manning a cannon after her husband was wounded.

Washington had ordered Greene's division to Freehold to protect the Continentals' right flank. After marching three miles, however, Greene received word of Lee's withdrawal. Without orders, Greene reversed his division's march, and at Combs Hill he placed his division with eight or ten cannon at its crest. The artillery bombarded the left wing of the British line and repulsed an attack led by General Cornwallis. James McHenry later wrote that "General Greene . . . gave the most evident and unequivocal marks of great military worth."[5]

By dusk the fighting had ended, with each side suffering over two hundred casualties, including dozens who died of sunstroke. Due to the rugged ground and thick woods, Washington decided against pursuing the British army, which reached Sandy Hook two days later and ferried to Long Island, Staten Island, and New York City. Instead, while the British army moved, the Continental forces went to White Plains, New York, and began to wait watchfully for the British army's next operation.

By this time, however, Greene had become upset over a letter from

Washington that seemed to admonish him for not reconnoitering more quickly to find a location for the army's camp. Washington's criticism stemmed from his desire to have Greene back at headquarters to aid the commander in chief in preparing strategy for the end of 1778. Responding to the criticism, as well as showing his frustration that Washington had not praised him for his efforts as quartermaster general, Greene asserted, "Your Excellency has made me very unhappy. I can submit very patiently to deserved censure; but it wounds my feelings exceedingly to meet with a rebuke for doing what I conceivd to be a proper part of my duty, and in the order of things." Soon, however, Washington relieved the tension when he wrote a letter to Greene praising his service and asserting, "[Y]ou retain the same hold of my affections that I have professed to allow you."[6]

Washington now expected that the French alliance would soon greatly benefit the United States. Indeed, a French fleet under Admiral d'Estaing arrived off Sandy Hook in July. Greene, however, advised against a blockade of Admiral Howe's fleet at New York Bay. Instead, he recommended that the French fleet go to Newport, Rhode Island, where it could act in conjunction with Gen. John Sullivan's Continental troops to capture the city and its British defenders. Greene also convinced Washington to allow him to lead one of two divisions comprised of Continentals and militia that would march to Rhode Island to bolster Sullivan's force. On July 30, the day after the French fleet anchored off the coast of Rhode Island, Greene arrived at Coventry. With the exception of a couple of hours in 1776, this was the first time Greene had been back to Rhode Island in three years. It provided him with a joyous reunion with Caty, who would soon give birth to their third child, Cornelia Lott Greene, and it gave the general an opportunity to see his two children, George and Martha, for the first time.

In early August, however, the British fleet under Admiral Howe sailed for Rhode Island. On August 10, d'Estaing disembarked four thousand French soldiers; but with Howe's fleet closing in, d'Estaing reembarked the French troops and sailed out of Narragansett Bay to give battle. When Howe finally decided to take on d'Estaing, a hurricane-force storm battered and scattered the fleets for sixty hours. The British fleet now set sail for New York to seek repairs, and the French fleet limped back to Rhode Island, where it arrived on August 20, the day after Sullivan's force began its assault on Newport. But instead of supporting the Americans' attack, d'Estaing decided to sail to Boston to repair his vessels. Sullivan, Greene, and other American officers were outraged and distraught at d'Estaing's decision. Sullivan sent Greene and Lafayette to meet with d'Estaing. When they reached the admiral's ship, a seasick Greene, using Lafayette as his interpreter, urged d'Estaing to return to Rhode Island. He noted that the French fleet could do repairs in a Rhode Island port as easily as at Boston. Perhaps fearing the entrapment of his fleet in Narragansett Bay and apparently feeling pressure from his officers, the admiral nevertheless decided to continue to Boston. After this, Sullivan, seeing victory being forfeited, wrote a strongly worded letter of protest to d'Estaing denouncing the French fleet's abandonment of the Rhode Island campaign. Despite significant misgivings about sending such a critical statement to America's important ally, Greene signed it along with several other officers. But he subsequently became alarmed at the strain the letter created in Franco-American relations, and with Washington's encouragement, he worked to restore harmony between the American and French officers.

On August 24 Sullivan's force of approximately 5,500 men withdrew to Butts Hill, near the north end of Aquidneck Island. With Greene in command of the right wing, in the early morning of August 29, British and Hessian troops encountered Sullivan's advance units. At mid-morning Greene proposed a full-scale attack on the British, but Sullivan rejected the idea. Even Greene later acknowledged that Sullivan "had taken the more prudent measure." When several British ships in Narragansett Bay began to shell the American position, Greene quickly got four cannon to bombard the British vessels. At approximately 2:00 p.m. the Hessians launched an attack on the American right wing. But the Americans under Greene repulsed the attack and launched a counteroffensive that sent the enemy into retreat. An exchange of cannon fire near evening ended the Battle of Rhode Island, which involved more than two hundred American casualties and nearly three hundred British and Hessian casualties. The next day Sullivan evacuated the island, and on September 1 General Clinton arrived with a large British force. As Greene noted, the Americans had left the island just in time.[7]

During the next two years, Greene, as quartermaster general, was principally involved in acquiring various supplies for the army while hyperinflation gripped the American economy and the Continental Congress provided insufficient funding. Complicating things further, in November 1778 the Congress created a committee to oversee the Quartermaster and Commissary Departments in response to their high costs, as well as to allegations of abuses and fraud. This was the situation in January 1779 when Greene went to Philadelphia to submit his budget needs to Congress while establishing or maintaining good relations with its members. Since the Congress had criticized the commissions paid to the quartermaster general, he proposed to the committee that Congress should pay a salary of three thousand pounds sterling and expenses to the quartermaster general; but he also asserted that he would resign as quartermaster general if Congress approved any lesser compensation. Upset by the criticism in Congress, Greene expected to be well compensated for holding a position that he later described as "humiliating to my military pride." It would take eighteen months, however, before Congress passed a regulating plan for the quartermaster general.[8]

Despite the problem of supplying the army, Greene found an extraordinary excess of food in Philadelphia. Attending a number of parties, he witnessed a great amount of extravagance. For example, the hosts of one dinner party served 160 dishes of food. Greene began to wonder at the civil-military dichotomy for supplies. He declared that the "growing avarice and a declining currency" were "poor materials to build an independence upon." Within a year he denounced the "great body of the people" for being "contracted, selfish, and illiberal."[9]

While in Philadelphia, Greene wrote to Washington about war strategy for 1779. He advocated three objectives: moving the army to New Jersey as the most favorable location for securing supplies; if possible, forcing the British out of New York; and launching a campaign in western Pennsylvania and western New York against the Iroquois, who had been waging a bloody war against white settlers since Burgoyne's surrender. Although Greene was certainly not the first person to urge such a campaign against the Iroquois, his ideas on where and how to conduct the campaign became almost a blueprint for the expedition of 1779 led by John Sullivan and James Clinton.

In April Greene, accompanied by Caty, who had arrived at the American camp in December, made another visit to Philadelphia to make an additional plea to Congress for funding. By this time, however, Greene faced an increasing number of complaints against him and the Quartermaster Department, especially regarding the commission that he received on purchases. In response, Greene declared that he would not do the tedious work of a quartermaster general unless adequately compensated, and then he attempted to resign. Moreover, Greene informed the Board of War that the logistics of supplying the army was not a science; different circumstances significantly affected the acquisition and distribution of supplies.

In addition, Greene asserted that those people who believed corruption was the principal reason for the army's supply problems had no understanding of the difficulties involved in logistical operations. He emphasized that nations needed to spend money in order to wage war. In short, Greene said, he found himself trapped in a position where he was criticized for developments beyond his control. To John Jay, the president of the Continental Congress, Greene complained that "injurious Imputations, however unjust, may reach our Reputation," and therefore he wished to be rid of the position and to be able to seek his immortal fame on the battlefield. Reiterating the sentiments he had expressed in 1778 when Congress had offered him the position, Greene declared to George Washington, "I will not sacrifice my Reputation for any consideration whatever. . . . I should be willing to serve in the Department I am in, for a proper consideration, if I could serve without loss of Reputation. . . . There is a great difference between . . . serving where you have a fair prospect of honor, and laurels, and where you have no prospect of either. . . . No body ever heard of a quarter Master in History as such or in relateing any brilliant Action." To James Duane, head of the Board of Treasury, Greene asserted that he considered it as "derogatory to serve" as quartermaster general. "[W]hile I am drudging in an Office from which I shall receive no honor, and very few thanks," he further lamented, "I am loosing an opportunity of doing justice to my military character. And what adds to my mortification is, that my present humiliating employment is improv'd to pave the way for others glory." After

NATHANAEL GREENE
This portrait of Nathanael Greene was painted at the end of the
Revolutionary War. *Nathanael Greene by Charles Willson Peale,
from life, 1783. Independence National Historical Park.*

GEORGE WASHINGTON

As the commander in chief of the Continental Army, Washington selected
Nathanael Greene to be the commander of the Southern Army in 1780.
George Washington by James Peale, after Charles Willson Peale, c. 1787–90.
Independence National Historical Park.

HENRY KNOX

Knox, a close friend of Greene, was in charge of artillery in the Continental Army, and he later became Secretary of War. *Henry Knox by Charles Willson Peale, from life, c. 1784. Independence National Historical Park.*

ARTEMAS WARD

Ward was the Continental Army's senior major general until his resignation in 1777. *Artemas Ward by Charles Willson Peale, from life, c. 1790–95. Independence National Historical Park.*

JOHN SULLIVAN

Sullivan was one of the Continental Army's original brigadier generals and was later promoted to major general. He commanded forces in several northern campaigns and was later the governor of New Hampshire. *John Sullivan by Richard Morrell Staigg, after John Trumbull, 1876. Independence National Historical Park.*

HORATIO GATES

Gates was the hero of Saratoga, but was subsequently in command of the American force that suffered a crushing defeat at the Battle of Camden in South Carolina in 1780. *Horatio Gates by Charles Willson Peale, from life, 1782. Independence National Historical Park.*

ANTHONY WAYNE
General "Mad Anthony" Wayne fought with distinction in northern and southern campaigns and was a close friend of Nathanael Greene. Eleven years after the end of the Revolutionary War he led the United States Army to victory over the Indians at the Battle of Fallen Timbers. *Anthony Wayne by James Sharples Senior, from life, 1796. Independence National Historical Park.*

HENRY LEE

"Light-Horse Harry" Lee, who came from a prominent Virginia family, was a skillful cavalry officer and the father of Confederate general Robert E. Lee. *Henry Lee by Charles Willson Peale, from life, c. 1782. Independence National Historical Park.*

BARON VON STEUBEN

Steuben was the most important foreign soldier in the Continental Army. *Frederick William Augustus, Baron von Steuben, by Charles Willson Peale, after Charles Willson Peale, 1781–82. Independence National Historical Park.*

DANIEL MORGAN

Morgan was an officer from Virginia who served in several northern campaigns during the War for Independence and then led American troops to victory at the Battle of the Cowpens in South Carolina in 1781. *Daniel Morgan by Charles Willson Peale, from life, c. 1794. Independence National Historical Park.*

WILLIAM WASHINGTON

Washington was a cousin of George Washington. He became the senior cavalry officer in the Southern Army under Greene. *William Washington by Charles Willson Peale, from life, 1781–82. Independence National Historical Park.*

JOHN EAGER HOWARD

Courageous and skillful, Howard became one of the finest officers in the Continental Army. After the Revolutionary War, he served as the governor of Maryland and as a United States senator. *John Eager Howard by Charles Willson Peale, from life, c. 1781–94. Independence National Historical Park.*

OTHO HOLLAND WILLIAMS

Williams was an outstanding officer from Maryland who rose to the rank of brigadier general and especially distinguished himself in several battles while serving in the Southern Army. *Otho Holland Williams by Charles Willson Peale, after Charles Willson Peale, 1782–84. Independence National Historical Park.*

THOMAS SUMTER

Sumter, "the Gamecock," was a prominent leader of partisan troops in the South. Following the War of Independence, he served as a U.S. congressman and senator from South Carolina. *Thomas Sumter by Rembrandt Peale, from life, 1795–96. Independence National Historical Park.*

CHARLES CORNWALLIS
Cornwallis volunteered to serve in America during the Revolutionary War and was commissioned as a major general in the British army. But his independent command in the South led him to surrender his army at Yorktown in 1781. *Charles Cornwallis, 1st Marquis Cornwallis. The Library of Virginia.*

CATHARINE LITTLEFIELD GREENE MILLER
This portrait of Caty Greene, the devoted wife of General Greene,
was painted late in her life. *Catharine Littlefield Greene Miller, c.
1809. Telfair Museum of Art, Savannah, Georgia.*

Washington again advised Congress of the difficulties of the position, Greene agreed to remain as quartermaster general. His desire to maintain his reputation as a self-sacrificing patriot was of crucial importance in making the decision. Nevertheless, he continued to be greatly disenchanted with his position.[10]

Several months later, when British detachments conducted raids into Connecticut and New Jersey, Washington sent troops to defend the areas. Greene wanted to command some of these forces. But Congress left his name off the list of officers who would lead the expeditions. Greene now wrote to all of the generals to request their opinions about his prerogative to assume a field command if he wished. Of the responses that have been found, six of the generals believed he did have that right. Four other generals, however, argued that his position as quartermaster general barred him from taking a field command. The two strongest dissenters were Lord Stirling and Arthur St. Clair. As major generals who were junior to Greene in seniority, they could lose their field commands to him. Much to Greene's dismay, Washington agreed with the latter group. The commander in chief asserted that Greene's command at the battles of Monmouth Courthouse and Rhode Island had been only special assignments. Washington's position on this issue made Greene even more determined to resign as quartermaster general as soon as possible and return to a field command. Otherwise, he felt, he would not be able to serve the revolution in a way that would bring him the historical reputation that he craved.

As 1779 neared an end, Greene recommended to Washington that the army make its winter camp at Jockey Hollow, New Jersey, which was several miles southwest of Morristown and was quite protected on the east by the Watchung Mountains. But on January 3, 1780, before the underfed and inadequately clothed army was completely encamped, a blizzard engulfed the area with sub-zero temperatures and a snowfall that eventually totaled four to six feet. Regarding the soldiers, Greene stated, "Poor Fellows! [T]hey exhibit a picture truly distressing. More than half naked, and above two thirds starved." Washington now imposed quotas on supplies from all New Jersey counties. But Greene's efforts to bring in the provisions and forage were hampered by several storms. Private Joseph Plumb Martin later asserted, "We were absolutely, literally starved. I do solemnly declare that I did not put a single morsel of victuals into my mouth for four days and as many nights, except a little black birch bark which I gnawed off a stick of wood, if that can be called victuals. I saw several of the men roast their old shoes and eat them, and I was afterwards informed by one of the officers' waiters, that some of the officers killed and ate a favorite little dog that belonged to one of them." Some soldiers also plundered nearby estates for food. "The Army," declared Greene, "is upon the eve of disbanding for want of Provisions." Indeed, he felt that the impassable roads were actually keeping the army together by preventing the soldiers from deserting. By January 12, however, the immediate crisis had ended. Nevertheless, during the following months Greene and the army continued to have to scrounge for food. Greene sarcastically noted that "a country overflowing with plenty are now suffering an army employed for the defense of everything that is dear and valuable to perish for lack of food."[11]

The basic problem in provisioning the army stemmed from the fact that the states were not providing funds to the national treasury to back the Continental currency, which inflation rendered almost valueless. To address this problem, Congress in late February passed a resolution that called for the states to pay directly for the expenses of their own lines in the Continental Army and provide the army with other needed supplies according to a quota system. This meant that Continental officers would no longer purchase goods, but instead would only receive and transport supplies. "The measure," asserted Greene, "seems to be calculated more for the convenience of each state, than for the accommodation of the service." He correctly predicted that the system would be a failure and that the Continental Army would have to requisition supplies by force and give certificates of credit in exchange for goods. Seeing the certificates as no better than the inflated currency, the public would accept them only because of social pressure or military intimidation.[12]

Greene learned from Philip Schuyler, who had been elected to Congress in November 1779, that the Rhode Islander's opponents in Congress constantly denounced him whenever issues regarding the Quartermaster Department were discussed. But Greene also had his supporters in Congress, including one who commented that he should succeed Washington if anything happened to the commander in chief. In late March, Greene and Caty, who had given birth to their fourth child two months earlier, a son named Nathanael Ray Greene, went to Philadelphia to meet with Congress. But because of his dislike of Thomas Mifflin, who was Washington's enemy, and his disapproval of the new plan for requisitioning supplies, Greene's comments were largely negative, and he failed to acknowledge the enormous problems faced by Congress. To Alexander McDougall, Greene asserted, "I have been among the great at Philadelphia and have a worse opinion of the issue of our cause than ever. . . . They are haughtier and more imperious than ever; and their subordinate Boards have all the insolence of office." Aware of Greene's disdain for Congress, some Congressional delegates believed it was time to replace him as quartermaster general.[13]

When Greene arrived back at the army's headquarters, he was ill and fed up with Congress. Nevertheless, he agreed to submit recommendations to a new committee headed by Schuyler for improving the Quartermaster Department. As Schuyler's committee soon informed Congress, the army was desperately short of all supplies. In early May, Greene declared, "Political bodies are often too tardy in their measures for the emergencies of War." Greene believed that the only solution was to hold a convention for creating a constitution that would grant Congress significant power to override the states in making measures to promote the national interest.[14]

As the lack of supplies continued and as five months passed without pay for the soldiers, feelings of anger and despair became prevalent in the army. At evening roll call on May 25 they culminated in mutiny when two regiments of the Connecticut Line expressed their dissatisfaction by acting contrary to orders, rudely talking to the officers, and then announcing they would either leave for home or use force to get more supplies.

Eventually, however, after much persuasion by officers, the Connecticut soldiers agreed to return to their huts. And Washington subsequently granted last-minute pardons to ten of eleven soldiers condemned to death, hoping that leniency would prevent any recurrence of the rebelliousness. Yet, Washington, Greene, and the other officers knew that a dangerous precedent had been established by the Connecticut Line at Jockey Hollow. If conditions did not improve, other Continental troops might follow the example of the Connecticut Line, and next time, the officers might not be able to control the situation. In fact, Greene later asserted that he was afraid the actions by the Connecticut troops "will run through the whole line like wild fire."[15]

A few days after the aborted mutiny, more bad news reached the American camp. A British expedition led by General Clinton had captured Charleston and the American army of 5,500 soldiers inside the city. This defeat was the result of a new strategy Britain had adopted in 1778 to focus its war effort on the South. After the Franco-American alliance of 1778, Britain found itself involved in a worldwide conflict, and it could no longer keep as many soldiers or ships in North America. Believing there was strong loyalist support in the South, which was seen as the most valuable area in North America because of its exports, British strategists had decided to concentrate on that region. In short, the British intended to Americanize the war. No longer would the British try to hold all colonial territory directly. Instead, the new plan called for liberating southern territory from rebel control and then quickly turning it over to the loyalists to defend. This would allow a small British force to move rapidly northward from a base of operation in East Florida and Georgia to conquer the entire South.

Despite all the problems, word arrived in the American camp that the French government would soon send an army of seven to ten thousand men and six ships-of-the-line to North America. But on June 6, General Knyphausen, who was in command in New York in Clinton's absence, led about six thousand men on a raid that resulted in the burning of Connecticut Farms. As militia blocked his advance to Springfield, Washington heard of the British action and moved the six Continental brigades from Jockey Hollow to an area near Springfield. For the next two weeks, the two armies closely watched each other. Then Washington heard that Clinton had arrived from South Carolina and was sailing up the Hudson River, which could endanger the American fort at West Point. The commander in chief now divided his army. As he marched most of the force toward West Point, Greene remained at Springfield with 2,500 soldiers and Henry Lee's cavalry.

On June 23, Knyphausen's force of six thousand left Elizabeth Town and advanced rapidly toward Connecticut Farms. As Greene's men withdrew before the substantially larger British force, Washington received reports of the action and sent Wayne's brigade to strike at the British right flank. The commander in chief also ordered the rest of the army to provide support to Greene's men by falling back toward Morristown. Meanwhile, Greene conducted a slow retreat and blocked each British effort to outflank the American troops. Eventually Greene's men had withdrawn beyond Springfield to the edge of the Short Hills, which provided the Americans with a more defensible terrain. The British then halted, burned more than twenty buildings in Springfield, and began a long retreat to Staten Island.

Within two weeks, after it had become clear that the British had abandoned any further offensive operations in New Jersey, the Americans proclaimed the Battle of Springfield an American victory and praised Greene for his leadership. Indeed, Greene's skilled retreat foreshadowed the successful campaign he would soon wage in the South.

On July 10 the vanguard of a large French force under the command of fifty-five-year-old General Comte de Rochambeau arrived at Newport, Rhode Island. Washington now considered a Franco-American operation against New York City, despite the large number of British troops in the city and the small front that the British would be defending. Greene, however, strongly opposed the proposed operation, which he described as "*Don Quixotal*," unless the French fleet could secure control of New York harbor. And this did not occur, because three days after the arrival of the French, a six-vessel reinforcement for the British fleet appeared off Sandy Hook.[16]

As the French arrived at Newport, Greene again expressed his dissatisfaction with his role as quartermaster general. He declared that for two years he had wanted to resign from the position but Congress would not consent and he could not force the issue "without hazzarding my reputation, and bringing the business into greater confusion, and the army into the greatest distress. Thus I have been draged on, contrary to my inclinations; and apprehend I shall not have it in my power to procure my discharge this campaign." But a few days later Greene received word that Congress on July 15 had finally enacted the reorganization plan for the Quartermaster Department. This plan was based on a cost-cutting approach that especially reduced the size of the Forage and Wagon Departments. Already greatly alarmed by the increased reliance on the states for supplies as established by Congress's resolution in February, Greene now criticized the elimination of key personnel, including his most talented assistants, and he argued that payment of fixed salaries rather than commissions would discourage men of talent from serving in the department. Greene also staunchly disagreed with the plan's assertion that the quartermaster general was responsible for the money spent by his deputies. Greene declared that he was not accountable for the financial actions of these men after Congress had appointed them to office.

Because of his vociferous dislike of various aspects of Congress's reorganization plan, which he believed would undermine the Quartermaster Department and ruin his reputation, Greene resigned as quartermaster general on July 26. He saw this as an honorable way to give up the position and to pursue laurels and historical fame as a field commander. As susceptible as any of his contemporaries to the eighteenth-century weakness for conspiracy theories, Greene had concluded that a Congressional cabal, led by Roger Sherman, was pursuing policies to restrict the Quartermaster Department and humiliate Greene. Later, however, Greene would find out that Sherman had actually supported him. Nevertheless, in August Greene argued that there was a group of Congressional conspirators who promoted policies meant to force him to resign. "This might not be the design of the greater part," declared Greene, "but I am perswaded it was the plan of a few."[17]

Although Congress accepted Greene's resignation, it became quite upset about several features of his decision to resign. Congress believed that Greene's resignation would hurt Franco-American operations in 1780, and it felt Greene had not given Congressional delegates an opportunity to address the defects that Greene saw in the new system. But most importantly, some Congressional members were outraged at the language Greene used in his letter of resignation. Denouncing his sarcastic comments, they were especially upset at the use of the word "Administration" to describe Congress, since this conjured up images of Britain's corrupt and arbitrary government.[18]

Soon, however, Congressional outrage over Greene's resignation had largely subsided. When British transports with eight thousand troops moved eastward through Long Island Sound to attack the French at Newport in late July, Washington rapidly marched his army in ninety-degree heat toward Kingsbridge to force Clinton to withdraw back to New York City. As the two armies engaged in this maneuvering, the situation concerning the Quartermaster Department became even more critical, since the Continental Army required a sufficient supply of goods. The Committee at Headquarters, which was a congressional committee at Jockey Hollow that evaluated the Quartermaster Department, requested that Greene temporarily stay on as quartermaster general to aid Washington during the campaign in 1780. Greene told the committee he would stay only if certain conditions were met, including the repeal of the act creating the new supply system, as well as the passing of a resolution granting regulatory power over the Quartermaster Department to Washington, the Committee at Headquarters, or both.

Congress exploded with indignation at Greene's response, seeing it as an attempt to dictate terms to Congress, which it essentially was. Congress even considered suspending Greene from his command in the line. Washington was alarmed enough by this talk that he warned Congress of the very detrimental results that would follow removal of Greene from his command. But, once more, Congress's outrage quickly died away, and Greene agreed to remain as quartermaster general for two weeks until his successor, Timothy Pickering, was able to assume control of the Department. On August 19 Joseph Reed wrote to Greene that he had few Congressional enemies. Nevertheless, Greene was greatly angered by the thought of Congress discussing the idea of stripping him of his rank. To Caty he wrote that it was "one of the most high handed and arbitrary measures that ever disgraced the Annals of a free people." Soon, however, Greene and Congress had moved beyond the bitter controversy.[19]

On September 17 Washington went to Hartford, Connecticut, to meet with the French commanders. During his absence, Washington left Greene in command of the Continental Army, which remained at Tappan to protect West Point against any British attack. But the British plan was to seize West Point by treachery, rather than force. Pressured by debt, passed over for promotion, unhappy about the alliance with Catholic France, and humiliated by a court-martial that resulted from his abuse of authority, Gen. Benedict Arnold negotiated with the British through Maj. John André to surrender West Point in exchange for a military commission and a very sizeable amount of money. The plan, however, fell through when André was captured with Arnold's plans for turning over the fort to the British. When Greene was informed of these developments, which he described as "treason . . . of the blackest kind," he made preparations to defend West Point. But the British did not attempt any action against the fortress.[20]

When Washington returned to Continental headquarters at the end of September, he appointed Greene to head the court that found André guilty of spying and sentenced him to be hanged. Subsequently, Greene also served as Washington's unofficial envoy to meet with a British delegation sent by General Clinton to save André from being executed. Greene, however, was authorized only to offer André in exchange for Arnold, a deal the British were unwilling to make. As a result, on October 2 André was hanged at Newburgh, New York. Shortly thereafter Greene assumed command at West Point.

As bad as the news was about Arnold's treachery, even worse was word from the South that an American army under Gen. Horatio Gates, which had been hastily assembled in the aftermath of the surrender of Benjamin Lincoln's army at Charleston, had been annihilated by British forces at Camden, South Carolina, on August 16. In short, the Americans had now lost two armies in South Carolina during a period of just over three months. Dismayed by the news and showing his long-standing antagonism toward Gates, Greene declared, "No man but [Gates] . . . in America, has the faculty of taking and loseing whole Armies." Yet, several months later, after having suffered the tribulations of commanding an army, he noted, "What little incidents either give or destroy reputation. How many long hours a man may labour with an honest zeal in his Countrys service and be disgracd for the most triffling error either in conduct or opinion. . . . Therefore it is necessary for a man to be fortunate as well as wise and just."[21]

Soon Greene was pleased to receive reports that Gates was to be removed from his command in the South and that the Rhode Islander would be selected to replace him. Since the spring of 1779, Greene had indicated an interest in the southern command. Now he reiterated that interest in a letter to the Committee at Headquarters. But as days went by with no word from Congress, Greene began to fear he would not be appointed to replace Gates. However, with Congressional delegates from three southern states urging the selection of Greene, Washington on October 14 appointed the thirty-eight-year-old Rhode Islander as the new commander of the Southern Army. During the previous five and a half years of service on and off the field, Greene had demonstrated to the commander in chief that he was a talented field commander, a skilled strategist, and a fine administrator. Washington felt that Greene was the best choice for the position, though the commander in chief noted, "In the command he is going into he will have every disadvantage to struggle with." Of a southern congressman Washington asked, "[W]hat can a General do, without men, without arms, without cloathing, without stores, without provisions?" Nevertheless, the selection of Greene was largely popular in the army. Gen. Robert Howe wrote, "Gen'l Greene will deserve success whether he obtains it or not." But any success or failure would stem directly from the Rhode Islander's decisions, since he now would be completely on his own as a commander. Washington reinforced this fact when he said to Greene, "I can give you no particular instructions but must leave you to govern yourself intirely according to your own prudence and judgment and the circumstances in which you find yourself." Those circumstances would soon place tremendous pressure on Greene's extensive abilities.[22]

A week before the Rhode Islander's appointment, the British had suffered a significant defeat in the South when General Cornwallis's loyalist left wing was wiped out by western frontiersmen at King's Mountain, thirty miles west of Charlotte and just inside the South Carolina border. This had hurt Cornwallis's plan to create an effective southern loyalist force, and it reinvigorated partisan resistance in South Carolina. Nevertheless, the victory would cause significant difficulties for Greene because it dissipated the sense of urgency among many southern leaders that had been created by the losses at Charleston and Camden. This would compound the problem of trying to obtain supplies for the Southern Army. Moreover, King's Mountain led many southern rebels to believe unrealistically that the British could be defeated by relying primarily on the militia. As Greene prepared to head south of the Mason-Dixon line for the first time in his life, even he did not fully appreciate the very problematic situation that he had inherited.

Mobility (1780–81)

WHEN GREENE learned that he had been appointed commander of the Southern Department, one of his greatest wartime ambitions was realized. But it also created major fears connected to his ambition. As he told Washington, "My only consolation is, that if I fail I hope it will not be accompanied with any marks of personal disgrace. Censure and reproach ever follow the unfortunate. This I expect if I don't succeed; [But] . . . [t]he ruin of my family is what hangs most heavy upon my mind. My fortune is small; and misfortune or disgrace to me, must be ruin to them." Indeed, Greene's thoughts now turned more than ever to his family. He desperately wanted to visit Caty and his children before proceeding southward, but the departure of British troops from New York, probably to cooperate with General Cornwallis's army in the southern states, forced him to leave for the South without seeing his family. In fact, Greene would not see his wife for two years, and it would be another year beyond that before he would see his children. To Caty he wrote, "How unfriendly is war to domestic happiness."[1]

Since the beginning of the Revolutionary War, Greene had been a fervent nationalist who denounced the "prejudices" of people with strong "local attachments." Soon after the fighting had started, he declared, "I feel the cause and not the place. I would as soon go to Virginia as stay" in New England. Now he would have the opportunity to serve the cause below the Potomac. On October 23 Greene left for the South. Within four days he had arrived in Philadelphia, where he would spend more than a week encouraging Congress to provide

SOUTHERN THEATER

the Southern Army with supplies and men. Greene emphasized that sufficient funding was of crucial importance. To Samuel Huntington, the president of the Continental Congress, he asserted, "Money is the Sinews of War, and without a Military Chest, it is next to impossible to employ an Army to effect; altho Troops may be levied and the great Articles provided to equip them for the Field, a thousand things essential to Success will occur in the course of Operations which cannot be foreseen or provided for." As his discussions with Congressional delegates came to an end, Greene declared, "They all promised fair, but I fear will do little: ability is wanting with some and inclination with others."[2]

When he resumed his journey southward, he was accompanied by General von Steuben, whom Washington had assigned as Inspector General of the Southern Army to help rebuild it. In Virginia, Greene and Steuben stayed at Mount Vernon, where Martha Washington served as their hostess. To one of his colleagues, Steuben made very critical remarks on the home's architecture. Greene, however, wrote to Washington that he thought the home was one of the most pleasant residences he had seen, and he declared that Steuben concurred, which meant that either Greene or Steuben was involved in telling a small social lie.

After meeting with leaders at Annapolis, Maryland, and Richmond, Virginia, to seek more supplies, Greene left Steuben in Virginia to head the effort against a British force that had recently arrived in the Chesapeake. Arriving in Charlotte, North Carolina, on December 2, Greene formally took command of the Southern Army the next day. He thus became its fourth commander in two years. Despite rumors of bad feelings between Greene and Gates, the latter displayed respect and cordiality toward the new commander. Greene, however, wrote to Joseph Reed that Gates "has lost the Confidence of the Officers; and the Troops all their Discipline: and so addicted to plundering that they were a terror to the Inhabitants." And when they were not robbing the local people, they were stealing from each other. In fact, the Southern Army was little better than an undisciplined, plundering mob. It was, wrote Greene, "but the shadow of an army in the midst of distress."[3]

Although Greene had anticipated major supply problems, he was shocked by the horrible conditions that he saw. Many soldiers were so close to naked they were unable to do even the most basic jobs. Indeed, a substantial number of the men wore just a blanket wrapped Indian-style about the waist. Moreover, the amount of ammunition was very low, and the army had only three days' worth of provisions. Of 2,307 Continentals and militia in the Southern Army, only about eight hundred were sufficiently equipped. To Governor Thomas Jefferson of Virginia, Greene wrote, "I find the Troops . . . in a most wretched Condition, destitute of every thing necessary either for the Comfort or Convenience of Soldiers." Beyond the failure of the Congress to provide supplies, this appalling situation was the result of drought in the highlands, floods in the lowlands, and drafting farmers into the militia.[4]

During his first night in camp, Greene discussed the issue of military supplies and local resources with Col. Thomas Polk, who later asserted that Greene soon had a better understanding of the supply situation than Gates did throughout his command. Greene quickly concluded that he had to order a sweeping reorganization of the Southern Army, including the selection of new men to the posts of adjutant general, quartermaster general, and commissary general. Furthermore, the Virginia cavalry was in such a deplorable condition that Greene ordered them to go home, and he wrote to Governor Jefferson that they were to return only after being properly supplied. Greene also wrote numerous letters to those who might be able to give assistance, and he ordered that all sheeting and osnaburg (a heavy coarse cotton in a plain weave) in the countryside be sent to seamstresses to be made into overalls. Because of a lack of funds, he recommended payment in salt for their services. Indeed, Greene insisted that the Southern Army not plunder or injure the civilians in any way, since he believed such restraint toward civilians would make friends for the American cause and promote the legitimacy of the United States.

Desertion was such a great problem that Greene court-martialed and sentenced to death the first deserter caught during his command, and the entire army was required to watch the execution. The stringent enforcement of the army's regulations led to discontent in the ranks. The night of the deserter's execution, one soldier bitterly complained, "It is new Lords, new laws." Nevertheless, Greene had set an example that began to lessen the problems with deserters.[5]

In the final months of 1780 British military operations in the South consisted of two fronts. A force in Virginia attempted to interrupt the southward flow of supplies and to establish a fort at the mouth of the James River to control shipping, while a larger army under General Cornwallis attempted to secure the Carolinas. Confronted with this British strategy, Alexander Martin, a member of the North Carolina Board of War, pressured Greene to establish immediately a line of outposts extending southward to the British position in South Carolina. But Greene, according to Martin, noted that it would take "some time to inform himself of the Country, not choozing to be in surprizing Distance of Lord Cornwallis until he was strong enough to fight him." As he familiarized himself with the Carolinas, Greene gathered information about the rivers and roads, which would benefit him in the campaign ahead.[6]

In addition, Greene had to deal with discontent among the officers. William Smallwood of Maryland, who had been promoted to major general on September 15, was accused by some officers of having spread rumors about Gates to further discredit him, and Gates and Greene believed that Smallwood had wanted to become the commander of the Southern Army. Moreover, Smallwood refused to serve if Baron von Steuben outranked him and assumed command of the Southern Army should anything happen to Greene. Smallwood wanted Greene to petition Congress to predate the Marylander's promotion to major general before that of Steuben. Greene absolutely refused, but he eventually gave permission to Smallwood to state his grievance before Congress.

Greene also pressured the North Carolina Board of War for Continental regiments, but it replied that for the near future he should use militias. Referring to the belief of some southern leaders that militia could bear the main burden of defeating Cornwallis, Greene declared, "Partizan strokes in war are like the garnish of a table, they give splendor to the Army and reputation to the Officers, but they afford no substantial national security. . . . You may strike a hundred strokes, and reap little benefit from them, unless you have a good Army to take advantage of your success. The enemy will never relinquish their plan, nor the people be firm in our favor untill they behold a better barrier on the field than a Volunteer Militia who are one day out and the next at home." Nevertheless, Greene recognized the militia's potential value. It could rapidly increase the size of his Continental force and independently harass the British. Indeed, the militia would be a significant part of Greene's southern strategy. To Francis Marion, the famed "Swamp Fox," he declared, "[W]e must endavour to keep up a Partizan War, and preserve the Tide of Sentiment among the People as much as possible in our Favour."[7]

As Greene prepared to march most of his army southward to the Pee Dee River in South Carolina, where supplies seemed to be more abundant, he made the crucial decision to split his force. This decision, which would shape the outcome of the conflict in the South, defied the classic military tenet that a commander should not divide his force when facing a numerically superior enemy. To facilitate obtaining sufficient resources for his troops and to prevent the British from concentrating their forces, Greene ordered Brig. Gen. Daniel Morgan of Virginia, a skilled rifleman and veteran of the French and Indian War who suffered from a serious arthritic condition, to lead approximately 350 infantry and Lt. Col. William Washington's cavalry southwestward to the Broad River, where they would be joined by militiamen. Morgan's troops were to gather supplies, harass the British, and win support from the local population. At the same time, Greene's force, in conjunction with Francis Marion's militia, could assault British garrisons and disrupt General Cornwallis's communications with Charleston. If Cornwallis moved against Greene, Morgan's troops could attack the rear of the British army and its outposts.

By dividing his army and coordinating it with actions by partisans in the Carolinas, Greene took the initiative away from Cornwallis and effectively encircled the British force. Although Greene knew that the partisans were potentially unreliable, he recognized that they were essential to an overall strategy against the British. In fact, Greene's great innovation during the war for independence was the coordinating of the movements of regular and partisan forces in a very mobile style of war, similar to Mao Tse-tung's and General Vo Nguyen Giap's campaigns nearly two centuries later, which often traded space for time. Foreshadowing one of Mao's principles for unconventional warfare, Greene understood that a willingness to run away is required of irregular troops. During the southern campaign, he asserted, "The first object in Civil and Military maxims is to preserve community from any capital misfortune." Forced into this Fabian strategy by time and necessity, the Rhode Islander used it to near perfection. But Greene, also like Mao, recognized that eventually, after the enemy has been debilitated by a long pursuit, there must be a concentration of forces to meet the enemy in a more orthodox type of warfare. It was this innovative approach to strategy that made Greene a revolutionary general in more ways than one. In particular, he became a harbinger of certain aspects of modern revolutionary war strategy.[8]

Five days before Christmas, the two parts of the Southern Army headed off to their different destinations. The initial movement, however, was slow because of very muddy roads resulting from eleven days of constant rain that had ended just before their departure. As a result, Greene's force did not reach the Pee Dee River until December 26. The men, including many who still had no clothing except for a blanket wrapped around the waist, established a camp and sought some relief. As Greene noted, "no army ever wanted it more." And to Morgan he wrote: "Our prospects with regards to provisions are mended, but this is no Egypt."[9]

Indeed, the Pee Dee River location only temporarily helped the supply situation. Three days after Christmas, Greene wrote to Washington, "I will not pain your Excellency with further accounts of the wants and sufferings of this army; but I am not without great apprehension of its entire dissolution." And two weeks later Greene complained to the commander in chief, "It is true I came to the Southward in expectation of meeting with difficulties but they far exceed what I had any Idea of." The locals were reluctant to offer supplies since the Southern Army had little to give in return. Therefore, Greene was forced to begin the confiscation of goods. To make matters worse, supplies sent southward for the army often were taken in raids by loyalist groups or appropriated by American agents. Furthermore, many soldiers were ill, and there was a constant fear of an outbreak of smallpox. As Greene evaluated the resources that he had for trying to build a viable Southern Army, he laconically noted, "This is really making bricks without straw."[10]

After the fall of Charleston, General Clinton had issued a proclamation that freed prisoners of war from parole and restored their citizenship rights if they swore an oath of allegiance to the King and supported the restoration of British rule in South Carolina. This measure, however, undermined the British effort, because it required South Carolinians to chose sides rather than sit out the war, and hard-line loyalists, feeling it was too lenient, began additional persecution of rebels and suspected rebels, which led to increased terror by both sides. In fact, the civil war between rebels and loyalists in the Carolinas became as vicious as the fighting anywhere between these groups during the Revolutionary War. Greene wrote to Caty, "Human misery has become a subject for sport and ridicule. With us the difference between Whig and Tory is little more than a division of sentiment; but here they persecute each other with little less than savage fury. . . . The sufferings and distress of the Inhabitants beggars all description, and requires the liveliest imagination to conceive the cruelties and devastations which prevail."[11]

At Winnsboro, Cornwallis divided his army in response to Greene's decision to split his army into two. The British commander then sent Lt. Col. Banastre Tarleton's legion of approximately one thousand men, consisting of dragoons, regular infantry, and loyalists, after Morgan. In addition, Maj. Gen. Alexander Leslie's 1,500 troops had arrived from the Chesapeake and would join Cornwallis's army. With this reinforcement, Cornwallis would keep watch on Greene's movements and be ready to finish off Morgan's force if needed.

Morgan, unable to outrace Tarleton, decided in mid-January 1781 to position his men at a place in South Carolina called the Cowpens, where cattle had once been rounded up. The area was a wide plain with several low hills in front of the Broad River, which would prevent any quick American retreat in battle. This meant Morgan was forcing his soldiers to stay and fight. Using a three-line battle formation, he had a screen of riflemen in front, backed by a second line of South Carolina militia, and, lastly, the Continentals and more riflemen. The light cavalry were held in reserve.

The impetuous and ruthless Tarleton ordered a frontal assault against Morgan's force. As the redcoats advanced, the first two American lines fired deadly volleys and then retreated. The third line initially gave way but then regrouped, and their bayonet charge along with the cavalry attacks on the flanks routed the enemy, as Tarleton lost more than 90 percent of his force. Only Tarleton, some cavalry, and his baggage guard escaped the disaster. The next day Morgan ordered his cavalry and most of the militiamen to march 702 British prisoners to the upper Catawba River, where other escorts would take them to Virginia. In short, Tarleton's debacle at the Cowpens had caused a serious setback for the British plan to Americanize the war in the South. With only seventy-two casualties, Morgan now began a march to rejoin Greene, who would partly base some of his own battlefield tactics on those Morgan had so successfully used at the Cowpens. As he had throughout his career, Greene assimilated proven methods into his approach to war.

When Leslie's troops and the remnants of Tarleton's force rejoined Cornwallis, he was determined to retake those captured at the Cowpens and get revenge for the humiliation of Tarleton's debacle. Leaving camp on January 19, he began a forced march to cut off Morgan before he could rejoin Greene. But a lack of good intelligence information sent him in the wrong direction since he thought Morgan was still at the Cowpens or had moved toward Ninety-Six. When Cornwallis realized his mistake, he burned or otherwise destroyed much of his baggage and supply train, including his own personal belongings and all the casks of rum, to move more quickly across muddy roads and icy, swollen streams in order to catch up with the fast-moving Morgan, who had covered more than a hundred miles in less than five marching days.

On January 23 word reached Greene's camp on the Pee Dee River that Morgan's force had won a stunning victory. Greene wrote to Washington that "[t]he event is glorious." As those at the Southern Army's headquarters celebrated, Greene considered a quick attack on the British outpost at Ninety-Six to prevent any further enemy action against Morgan. Greene realized, however, that this was not feasible since the Virginia militia was preparing to go home soon, when its enlistments expired, and overall his force was in a "wretched condition." Instead, he decided to reunite the two parts of the Southern Army at Salisbury, retreat into North Carolina, and, if necessary, escape temporarily into Virginia across the Dan River. Greene soon stated that he was "not without hopes of ruining Lord Cornwallis if he persists in his mad scheme of pushing through the Country." The American retreat would bring the Southern Army ever closer to needed supplies in Virginia, while stretching the British supply lines to the breaking point. Greene intended to wait for the right moment, then turn against the overstretched British force.[12]

With just a guard of dragoons and a guide, Greene traveled more than one hundred miles to meet with Morgan at Beattie's Ford on the Catawba River during the afternoon of January 31. But around the time that Greene arrived, the vanguard of Cornwallis's army reached the opposite side of the swollen river. Later that day, as the water level of the Catawba River began to drop, Morgan's infantry marched through deep mud toward the Yadkin River and Salisbury. This left approximately five hundred militiamen to defend the Catawba fords where the British could cross. Astutely analyzing British intentions and the militia's potentially vulnerable position, Greene recommended to Gen. William L. Davidson that he take 250 men to Cowan's Ford, which was about five hundred yards wide, with fast running water about three to four feet deep. Against Greene's advice, however, Davidson kept only two dozen soldiers at the river, while the rest were about three quarters of a mile away.

The British would make Davidson pay for failing to heed Greene's tactical advice. At 1:00 a.m. the next morning Cornwallis launched an attack across the Catawba. When Davidson was fatally wounded in the chest, the demoralized militiamen were routed. Greene vainly awaited the arrival of the militia at a designated rendezvous location about sixteen miles from where the British had crossed the river. When it became apparent that the militiamen had been scattered, Greene rode off to Salisbury, where he sent word to Gen. Isaac Huger, who was in command of the Southern Army during Greene's absence, that he should unite his force with Morgan's at Guilford Court House unless he was already across the Yadkin River and within twenty-four hours of Salisbury.

Greene wanted to draw Cornwallis an even greater distance away from his supply depots, but the hard-charging British general, who now burned more of his army's baggage, almost caught up with Morgan at the Yadkin River. Morgan's force, however, was able to escape across the swollen river on February 2 by using the only boats in the area. The lack of boats and the river's water level prevented Cornwallis from sending his troops across the Yadkin for two days. Nevertheless, British scouts using canoes were able to determine that Greene intended to join his forces together at Guilford Court House and then retreat northward across the Dan River into Virginia. Cornwallis was now determined to prevent Greene from escaping across the Dan.

The ragged and hungry American troops trudged through a continuous rain to reach Guilford Court House, where Greene held a council of war on February 9 that included Morgan, Huger, and Col. Otho Williams of Maryland. A month earlier Greene had declared to Alexander Hamilton that he did not hold councils of war. However, the Rhode Islander knew that abandoning North Carolina could jeopardize his reputation. He probably wanted the council to sanction the retreat to Virginia, which he had already decided was essential for the survival of the army. To justify this action, Greene told the council that the Southern Army consisted of 2,026 badly armed regulars and militiamen, while Cornwallis had 2,500–3,000 troops. As Greene had hoped, the council unanimously decided to avoid an action against the British and to continue the Southern Army's retreat toward Virginia. "If I should risque a General action in our present situation," Greene wrote to Gen. Thomas Sumter, "we stand ten chances to one of getting defeated, & if defeated all the Southern States must fall." To Governor Abner Nash of North Carolina, Greene asserted, "Our force is so unequal to the enemy, as well in numbers as condition that it is the unanimous opinion of a Council of war held this day, that it would be inevitable ruin to the Army and no less ruinous to the American cause to hazard a General action; and therefore have advisd to our crossing the Dan River immediately."[13]

With Cornwallis just twenty-five miles away, Greene was the same distance from the shallow fords of the upper Dan River. The final leg of the race to the Dan might very well determine which side would win the war in the South. Greene thus ordered Col. Edward Carrington to assemble boats on the lower Dan, while ordering Williams to lead an elite force of seven hundred soldiers, including William Washington's cavalry and John Eager Howard's infantry, to protect the army and convince Cornwallis that the American retreat was toward the upper river. Greene's deception worked, as Cornwallis believed that Williams' movement indicated that the rebel force was heading for the upper Dan. For five days the Southern Army, with the British vanguard at times within sight of the American rearguard, sped toward the Virginia border. Finally, on February 13–14 the exhausted and tattered army used the boats assembled by Carrington to escape across the lower Dan into Virginia. Again motivated by adversity, Greene had won the race to the Dan. Once more he had successfully traded space for time.

Short of supplies and provisions, 150 miles from his main base of supplies, and too weak to venture immediately into the rebel stronghold of Virginia, Cornwallis retreated to Hillsboro and called on North Carolina loyalists to join him. But as Cornwallis noted to Lord Germain, the loyalist "numbers are not so great as had been represented and . . . their friendship . . . only passive." Meanwhile, Greene's army enjoyed an abundant supply of food in Halifax County, Virginia. As his army rested and gathered supplies, Greene came to believe that Cornwallis would soon enter Virginia, perhaps try to engage the Southern Army in battle, and eventually attempt to link up with the British force under the command of Benedict Arnold, the former rebel hero who had betrayed the American cause six months earlier. Greene decided the time was right to recross the Dan and strike at the British army, which was so far from its supply base. He asserted, "I am not without hopes of giving Lord Cornwallis a run in turn. At any rate I shall attempt to gall his rear." To allow him to conduct such an action, Greene requested that Governor Jefferson and Governor Nash call out their states' militias, and he asked Jefferson to grant Greene emergency powers to bypass some legal procedures.[14]

Thus, on February 18 Greene ordered Lee's legion and two companies of Maryland Continentals to assist Gen. Andrew Pickens's militia from North and South Carolina, which had just arrived near the Dan, as it attempted to harass the enemy's communications and foraging activities. Two days later Greene sent Williams's light infantry south of the Dan to stay between the Southern Army and Cornwallis's force in order to harass the British if they retreated toward their supply depot at Wilmington. Greene followed and met with Lee and Pickens close to the road that ran toward Hillsboro to inform them that he would soon send his entire army back across the Dan toward Guilford Court House. Shortly thereafter, Lee's and Pickens's forces surprised three hundred loyalists, who suffered 80 percent casualties. This thoroughly undermined Cornwallis's effort to gain loyalist recruits.

On February 25, Greene, whose army was now reinforced with six hundred Virginia militia, led the American force across the Dan to join Lee's cavalry and the Maryland Continentals near Hillsboro. As a result, Cornwallis decided to move against the Southern Army before more militia arrived to support Greene, and on March 6 the British advanced toward the American camp on the Haw River. As Greene moved most of the Southern Army to a new campsite at the ironworks on Troublesome Creek, Williams's force became involved in a running action with the British, which cost each side approximately twenty casualties.

During the next week, both armies remained on the move, as Greene seldom stayed two nights at the same location. Having decided not to confront Cornwallis until he had a numerically superior force, Greene saw 1,700 Virginia militiamen, 1,060 North Carolina militiamen, and four hundred Continentals join the Southern Army. Yet Greene noted that the militiamen "go and come." Nevertheless, in the short run he had approximately 4,400 troops. Greene thus began to reorganize his army and make preparations for striking at Cornwallis's force of 1,900 seasoned regulars before the American militiamen's six-week commitments had expired and reinforcements arrived at the British camp. Greene intended to confront Cornwallis in a conventional fight on a battleground of Greene's choosing. The Rhode Islander knew that the British could be defeated in such a battle, and that this would result in the collapse of Cornwallis's command. Even a British triumph, according to Greene, would be a Pyrrhic victory that would further undermine Cornwallis's small and undersupplied force. The Rhode Islander later wrote to George Washington, "[T]he great advantages which would result from the action, if we were victorious, and the little injury if we were otherwise, determind me to bring on an action as soon as possible." Therefore, Greene, despite being exhausted and suffering from a flare-up of his old eye problem, led the Southern Army along Troublesome Creek and through very settled farmland toward Guilford Court House, which he reached on March 14. During the retreat to the Dan in February, Greene had concluded that this area made a good location for fighting the British.[15]

Cornwallis, having received information that Greene's force had reached Guilford Court House about twelve miles away, decided to attack the Americans, even though British intelligence wrongly concluded that Greene's force totaled nine to ten thousand troops. At daybreak on a cold but crisp March 15 the British marched up Salisbury Road toward Guilford Court House.

After providing the soldiers with breakfast and rum, Greene dispersed his troops in battle formation, as he awaited the arrival of Cornwallis's rapidly advancing army. Greene largely adhered to Morgan's advice to deploy his troops much as the Old Wagoner had at the Cowpens. In particular, Greene used a three-line formation, which included the North Carolina militia in front, flanked by Lee's and Washington's cavalry. About four hundred yards behind was the Virginia militia, including a number of men who had served in the Continental Army. (Their commander was Gen. Edward Stevens, who had been humiliated when the Virginia militia had fled at Camden. Stevens now placed forty riflemen behind the militiamen with orders to shoot any who tried to flee.) And Continentals, who were the finest troops in the army, comprised the third line approximately 550 yards behind the Virginia militia. Greene took the tactical risk of holding no troops in reserve. Riding among the North Carolina militia before the battle began, Greene encouraged the men to fire at least two shots before falling back. But unlike the open terrain at the Cowpens, the setting of the Battle of Guilford Court House was a densely forested area that was broken by just a few clearings. This did seem to offset the battlefield tactics that the British favored, but Greene would not be able to view the first two lines from his position with the Continentals once the battle started.

By 1:30 p.m. Cornwallis had positioned his own force of 1,900 men, including Lt. Col. James Webster's brigade on the left of the road heading to Guilford Court House; Gen. Alexander Leslie's brigade on the right; and three six-pounders in the center. In reserve was

Tarleton's cavalry and Gen. Charles O'Hara's brigade. The battle began with a twenty-minute cannonade. Then, as the British troops advanced, the North Carolina militia began some uneven firing of muskets from a distance of 150 yards. When the redcoats got to within forty yards of the American position, they saw the militia with muskets aimed at them across a fence. Initially both sides paused and surveyed the situation. Then, with Webster encouraging his troops, the British advanced with muskets lowered at the bayonet charge position. The militiamen on both flanks, who felt protected by Lee's and Washington's cavalry, fired a devastating volley, but the North Carolinians in the middle immediately fled while throwing away muskets, knapsacks, and anything else that hindered their flight. Additional militiamen, particularly those on the right flank, began to flee after firing their second volley. The American officers, including Lee, vainly tried to halt the panicky stampede. Meanwhile, militiamen on the left flank held, until the British began to climb the fence. As the North Carolinians gave way, Washington's units withdrew in an orderly fashion to the right flank of the second line of militia, but Lee's force fell back to a wooded hill a half-mile away from the road.

The North Carolina militia had fled toward the flanks, which meant that the oncoming British were rushing toward the second American line. Greene and Stevens, anticipating that some of the North Carolinians might flee before firing two shots, had told the Virginia militia to allow the retreating Americans through their line. And the second line held, as many used trees for cover. The British faced such intense fighting that Cornwallis committed his reserves to the battle. Under constant attack, as Stevens was wounded in the thigh, the American right wing swung back until it was at a right angle to the rest of the line, which fought off three bayonet attacks. Cornwallis, despite having his horse being killed beneath him, led the final attack that finally broke the Virginians' resistance. With rumors of British to their rear, the Virginia militiamen fled in many directions. The way was now open for Cornwallis's troops to strike at the Continentals, who comprised the final American line.

Greene moved along the line of Continentals encouraging them to give the final blow to the enemy. But he would wait for their attack rather than risk a charge like Morgan's at the Cowpens; Greene had no intention of gambling with his army's existence. The British attacked the First Maryland Regiment, but, when Lieutenant Colonel Webster suffered a fatal wound through his knee, the redcoats were driven back. At this point the British placed two cannon on a small knoll, which Greene had failed to occupy, that was approximately 250 yards from the courthouse. When the redcoats renewed the assault, the Second Maryland Regiment, comprised of raw recruits, began to flee. With Col. John Gunby trapped beneath his dead horse, Lt. Col. John Eager Howard, one of the finest officers in the Continental ranks, used a short-range volley and a bayonet charge, along with a cavalry charge led by Washington, to stall the British attack and force the redcoats to seek protection from their artillery. Cornwallis unsuccessfully attempted to rally his men; so, to stop the American advance he resorted to the extreme measure of ordering his artillery to shoot grapeshot into the area where American and British soldiers were fighting, which led to a number of casualties on both sides.

The tactic, however, did stop the American assault and buy time for two British regiments to arrive as reinforcements. The American troops led by Howard and Washington were forced to retreat. Greene now ordered a general withdrawal toward the Speedwell Iron Works on Troublesome Creek, as Huger's Continentals protected the Southern Army's rear. Since the draught horses had been killed, the Americans, who suffered approximately 260 casualties, were forced to abandon their artillery as they withdrew. His numerous casualties, which were about double those of Greene's force, prevented Cornwallis from aggressively pursuing the Americans, though some fighting did continue for a while on the fringes and in isolated engagements. After ninety minutes, the Battle of Guilford Court House had ended in a Pyrrhic victory for the British, but Cornwallis had also very clearly lost the campaign in the Carolinas.

Nevertheless, Greene was highly critical of the militias' performance in the battle, which prompted Joseph Reed to warn him that this attitude could alienate people throughout the country who were supportive of the militias. Reed recommended to Greene that he adopt an attitude toward the militias like that one should have regarding a wife: "Be to their Faults a little blind And to their Virtues very kind." Greene, however, would continue to hold a negative view of the militias, even as they provided essential troops for his mobile war against the British.[16]

After the battle, as torrential rain saturated the area, Cornwallis rested his men at Guilford Court House, and Greene directed the construction of defensive works at Troublesome Creek, since he believed Cornwallis might order another assault. The British general, however, had suffered too many casualties, including twenty-eight officers, to consider a follow-up attack. As Cornwallis prepared to lead his army toward Cross Creek on Cape Fear River, he left about seventy of his worst wounded at New Garden, and he requested that Greene provide what care he could for them. Greene subsequently dispatched Lee's legion and a corps of riflemen to follow the British force, which now totaled about 1,400 troops. On March 20 Greene led the rest of his army, which had been abandoned by most of the militiamen, in pursuit of Cornwallis, who eventually decided to push on to Wilmington to find more supplies and a better defensive location.

By March 29 Greene had daringly decided to abandon his pursuit of Cornwallis and the defense of Virginia and instead to march his army to South Carolina. Writing to George Washington, Greene explained that remaining in North Carolina would simply allow the British to retain control of their posts throughout the Carolinas. But he believed that Cornwallis would probably follow the Southern Army when it went to South Carolina, which would allow Greene an opportunity to take a decisive action against the depleted British force. If, however, Cornwallis stayed in North Carolina, the Southern Army could seize the British posts in the Gamecock State. Greene declared: "The Manoeuvre will be critical and dangerous; and the troops exposed to every hardship. . . . I shall take every measure to avoid a misfortune; but necessity obliges me to commit myself to chance and I trust my friends will do justice to my reputation if any accident attends me." In short, as Greene remained concerned about how his leadership efforts in the South would define his reputation, his daring strategic vision for winning in the southern states drove him to return to South Carolina to end the campaign with an American victory.[17]

Endgame (1781–83)

Y LEADING his army to South Carolina while leaving a
British army almost totally unchallenged at his rear, Greene was again
violating a basic military tenet. To a North Carolina officer, he stated,
"Dont be surprisd if my movements dont correspond with your Ideas
of military propriety. War is an intricate business, and people are often savd by ways and means they least look for or expect." To defeat
the British in South Carolina, Greene once more would have to use
partisan forces. Making the most of his modest number of troops,
Greene ordered General Sumter to join him for action against Camden,
and he told General Pickens to besiege Ninety-Six. Furthermore, he
ordered General Marion to join Lee and capture Britain's intermedi-
ate posts and sever communications and supply lines between Camden
and Charleston. To accomplish this, however, he told Sumter, "[T]he
object must be a secret to all except the Generals; otherwise the Enemy will take measures to counteract us."[1]

But the situation became more complicated than Greene had expected. Cornwallis did not stay in North Carolina or march to South
Carolina; instead, he eventually led his army toward Virginia, which
was part of Greene's Southern Department command, to link up with
General Arnold's and Gen. William Phillips's forces in the Chesapeake.

To counter the increased British presence in the Chesapeake, Greene informed Lafayette, who had gone to Maryland, of the situation, and urged him to return as quickly as possible to Virginia. Since he was far from the theater of action, however, Greene could only give general advice regarding strategy in Virginia. Moreover, when Greene arrived near Camden he found it had stronger fortifications and more troops than he had anticipated. So, having placed his army at Hobkirk's Hill about a mile and a half north of Camden, he tried to starve the British into submission by preventing supplies from reaching Camden. He was unable, however, to cut off all supplies, partly because Sumter failed to use his militia to block supplies coming from the south and southwest. Greene remarked that "Camden seems to have some evil genius about it. What ever is attempted near that place is unfortunate." Nevertheless, twenty-six-year-old Lt. Col. Lord Francis Rawdon, the gangly but skillful British commander at Camden who had served in America since 1775, decided in April that he must crush Greene's force or eventually be defeated by the Southern Army. Receiving information from an American deserter that the Rhode Islander had sent his cannon to the rear, Rawdon made plans to attack Greene at Hobkirk's Hill.[2]

The Great Road that ran to Charleston cut across Hobkirk's Hill, with many trees on both sides, which gave cover to Greene's troops controlling its summit. But at approximately 11:00 a.m. on April 25 the troops were at various activities and Greene was having a cup of coffee in his tent, when British troops, which included every soldier under Rawdon's command who could be armed, rapidly advanced on the American position. As pickets opened fire, Greene quickly gained control of the situation. His troops had pitched camp in battle lines on the hill's slope, which allowed most of them to assemble quickly in battle formation. As Rawdon's most forward units moved along a narrow front between the trees, Capt. Robert Kirkwood's Delaware Continentals attempted to delay their advance. The British were attacking uphill. Nevertheless, recognizing the narrow British front, Greene ambitiously decided to orchestrate a double envelopment of Rawdon's force. To prevent the British troops from escaping the entrapment, he ordered Washington's dragoons to attack the enemy's rear. Washington's cavalrymen, however, after a very long ride around dense underbrush, found themselves far behind the main fighting. As they made prisoners of many noncombatants, wounded, and stragglers, Washington's dragoons lost valuable time for moving against the British battle line. Meanwhile, Rawdon, perceiving Greene's tactic, had quickly extended his first line by bringing forward units from the second line. Yet Greene's army seemed to have stopped the British advance, as American artillery, which had recently arrived, devastated the enemy line by firing grapeshot at short range.

But the battle soon turned in favor of the British, as confusion arose among the advancing American regiments. Capt. William Beatty of Col. John Gunby's crack First Maryland Regiment was killed, which threw the right flank of the regiment into disorder. As Gunby ordered a movement in support of the flank, the British, sensing disorder, forged ahead with a bayonet charge, causing the full regiment to retreat. Col. Benjamin Ford, commander of the Second Maryland Regiment, was struck down, and his troops fled. As a result, the First Virginia Regiment also fled. This allowed the British to attack the flank of Lt. Col. Samuel Hawes's Second Virginia Regiment, which had remained steady. Greene, who was with Hawes's regiment, continuously exposed himself to fire as he encouraged the troops. But fearing that the Virginians would be outflanked, Greene ordered the regiment's withdrawal. At this time, Washington returned from the enemy's rear, as Rawdon's troops were attempting to seize the American artillery. Hastily paroling the British captives, Washington and his dragoons raced to the aid of the artillery crews. After driving off the attackers, the dragoons quickly hitched horses to field pieces and took them away as a part of the general American retreat.

Despite suffering 268 losses, including 132 casualties, Greene was able to bring his army back together about three miles from the battlefield. Later that day the Southern Army withdrew another three miles before making camp. (Among the British soldiers who had been captured were four deserters from the Southern Army. All were sentenced to be hanged, and Greene approved of the court's decision.) Although the British were in control of Hobkirk's Hill, Rawdon had lost nearly 260 men, which was almost a third of his force. In fact, the outcome of the battle did not change the strategic situation, since Greene's army remained intact and could continue to endanger Rawdon's supply line.

To Steuben, Greene asserted, "This repulse, if such it may be called, will make no alteration in our general plan of operations." And to the Chevalier de La Luzerne, Greene succinctly stated the determination of the Southern Army when he wrote, "We fight get beat rise and fight again."[3]

On May 10 Rawdon evacuated Camden in order to defend Charleston against Greene. As Rawdon's force retreated southeastward, Lee, Marion, and Sumter captured the British support posts at Orangeburg, McCord's Ferry, and Friday's Ferry. They also forced the evacuation of the outposts at Nelson's Ferry and Georgetown. Thus, by early June the Americans controlled the northern and central parts of South Carolina. Also in late May and early June, three British forts in Georgia fell to Continentals led by Henry Lee and militia led by Pickens. After the interior of Georgia came under American control, Greene dispatched Joseph Clay, the paymaster of the Southern Army, to resurrect the Georgia state government.

Since Pickens's small force had been unable to capture Ninety-Six, Greene, on May 22, began a siege of the British outpost with its 550 loyalists. The town, however, was enclosed by a ditch, an abatis, and a stockade buttressed by dirt. Nearby was another fort with two blockhouses that could help protect the rivulet that provided water for the town. Ironically, Rawdon had ordered the evacuation of the post, but the messengers had been captured; Col. John Cruger, the loyalist commander, had strengthened rather than abandoned the post. Greene thus encountered another fortress that was better defended than he had anticipated. Nevertheless, he attempted a variety of tactics in the sweltering heat. His troops began digging a tunnel to undermine the stockade wall, but in a daring raid, a group of loyalists destroyed it before it was finished. Greene's troops also built a tower to shoot over the stockade wall. The fort's defenders, however, countered this by using sandbags to raise the height of the wall. Greene even ordered flaming arrows to be shot into the fort, but the loyalists pulled shingles off the roofs to keep them from burning. Finally, on June 18, an American assault broke into one of the fortifications, but a spirited counterattack drove it out. The next day Greene received word that William Washington and Sumter could not delay Rawdon's relief force of two thousand soldiers as it approached Ninety-Six. Therefore, Greene abandoned the siege after twenty-eight days.

Initially Greene hoped to gather militia and partisans to strike at Rawdon before he reached the post. When that plan fell through, the Rhode Islander withdrew his army northward. Using the same strategy he had used against Cornwallis several months earlier, he put as many rivers as possible between his weak forces and Rawdon's reinforced army. As a result, the British commander soon gave up the pursuit and returned to Ninety-Six.

Greene blamed the Virginia government for the failure of the siege because it had refused to adhere to his order to send two thousand militiamen to aid the Southern Army. To the Articles of Confederation Congress, Greene asserted that state leaders did not have the right to ignore a Continental commander's orders. This could have led to an important discussion of state-national relations, but the Congress refused to debate the issue, and Greene did not pursue the matter, feeling that his reputation was upheld when Rawdon abandoned Ninety-Six on July 3. Recognizing that Ninety-Six, like Camden, would continue to be susceptible to sieges from Greene's army, the British commander had decided that the abandonment of the post and the evacuation of the area's loyalists were the best strategy.

When Rawdon withdrew and divided his army by placing most of the troops under the command of Alexander Stewart, Greene led the Southern Army back to South Carolina. He hoped to attack Rawdon's force before it was reunited with Stewart's troops at Orangeburg. When that plan failed, Greene in mid-July took his men to the High Hills of the Santee River to rest them during the dog days of summer and to await a better opportunity to strike at the enemy. Meanwhile, a very frail Rawdon, who was exhausted by the summer campaign, returned to Britain on July 20 and left Stewart in command of the British and loyalist forces in South Carolina.

Soon after the Southern Army established its camp at the High Hills of the Santee, Governor Rutledge joined Greene to create a plan for reestablishing a civil government in the state. Writing to his wife about the great destruction that armies and outlaws had caused in South Carolina, Greene declared: "Here turn which way you will, you have nothing but the mournful widow, and the plaints of the fatherless Child; and behold nothing but houses desolated, and plantations laid waste. Ruin is in every form, and misery in every shape."[4]

Greene encouraged Sumter to lead militiamen against outposts at the rear of the British army. What was later referred to as the "Dog Days Expedition," did have some success, but failed to capture the six hundred enemy troops at Biggin Church. Although Greene publicly praised Sumter, he privately criticized a number of the South Carolinian's tactical decisions. This placed even more stress on their relationship, which had become strained by Sumter's failure to block supplies from reaching the British or to comply with Greene's requests for supplies. Nevertheless, as Greene noted, "We have had a severe campaign and tho fortune has been little our friend we have maintained our ground."[5]

Throughout August Greene pleaded with Congress's Board of War for more supplies, successfully encouraged a reorganizing of the South Carolina militia, promoted the recruitment of more cavalry in South Carolina, and sought reinforcements for the Southern Army from various sources. Greene thus expanded his army to more than two thousand well-rested troops, though this was fewer than he wanted.

While the Southern Army remained in the High Hills of the Santee, the British executed an American militia colonel who had broken his parole oath that disallowed any fighting against the Crown's forces. Although Greene was outraged and even briefly considered executing the next high-ranking British officer who became a prisoner of war, his attention was soon directed elsewhere when Stewart led his army out of Charleston. Despite harassment from the American cavalry, by late August the British commander had reached Eutaw Springs, which was named for two springs that flowed into Eutaw Creek and was located near the road that ran from Nelson's Ferry to Monck's Corner. Stewart encamped in an eight-acre clearing that was largely surrounded by oaks and cypresses.

This time there would be no American retreat, as Greene broke camp on August 23 to move against Stewart's army. Having become somewhat impatient, the Rhode Islander would be striking at an enemy force that was approximately the same size as his own. Two weeks later, on September 8, the Southern Army prepared to catch the British by surprise, as Greene led his troops at 4:00 a.m. seven miles from Burdell's Plantation to strike at Stewart's unsuspecting force still encamped at Eutaw Springs. So many defections had occurred on both sides that Greene later noted, "[W]e fought the enemy with British soldiers and they fought us with those of America."[6]

At about 7:00 a.m., after two American deserters informed Stewart that Greene's army was nearby, the British commander dispatched 150 troops to bring back 350 unarmed foragers who had been digging for sweet potatoes. However, the British troops encountered the vanguard of Greene's force, which comprised Lee's Legion of cavalry and infantry and South Carolina militiamen. A short skirmish drove back the British soldiers. But soon Stewart deployed his two thousand British and loyalist troops, as well as three artillery pieces, in a long line from Eutaw Creek to the woods south of River Road. Greene countered this with a two-line formation of 2,200 troops. As was his usual tactic, he placed the militiamen in the front line—North Carolina and South Carolina soldiers under Pickens and Marion. Greene also gave two three-pounder artillery pieces to the militia. In the second line he put Maryland, Virginia, and North Carolina Continentals. And he positioned Washington's cavalry and the Delaware Continentals as reserve forces.

As the Americans advanced, the militia, fighting like veteran troops, fired perhaps as many as seventeen rounds. Praising their performance later, Greene said they had fought like the veterans of "the great King of Prussia." But a bayonet charge by Stewart's men finally sent the militia in the center and on the right into a disorderly retreat. Greene quickly ordered the North Carolina Continentals to fill the gap in the first line. When the enemy troops fell back and were bolstered by Stewart's reserves, Greene ordered the Virginia and Maryland Continentals to fire and conduct a bayonet attack against the line, while Lee's Legion struck at Stewart's left flank and Washington's cavalry struck at the right. Soon the entire enemy line, except the British regulars under Maj. John Majoribanks, had fled. Greene now believed that the dislodgement of this last part of the enemy line would seal the American victory. He thus ordered Washington's cavalry to drive off Majoribanks's troops. But as Washington's dragoons wheeled around an impenetrable thicket they rode right into Majoribanks's well-fortified position. Over half of the dragoons were killed, wounded, or captured. And Washington, pinned under his wounded horse, was bayoneted and captured.[7]

As wounded and riderless horses coursed the area and the British used bayonets to kill unhorsed riders, Greene sent the Delaware Continentals to strike at Majoribanks's force. Faced with the furious charge of Kirkwood's men, the British troops withdrew. Indeed, the entire enemy army seemed to be in full retreat. Meanwhile, however, loyalists had barricaded themselves in a two-story brick house northeast of the British camp. Greene therefore directed many regulars to besiege the house. But as had happened at the Chew House during the Battle of Germantown, the enemy troops were able to cause numerous casualties by pouring fire down on the American soldiers. In addition, great disorder soon arose among many other American troops, as they began to plunder the supplies of food and liquor in the abandoned British camp. Recognizing the opportunity, Majoribanks now led his troops in an attack on the Americans in the British camp, which routed Greene's men. And as Stewart rallied some of the retreating British troops, he was able to return to the battlefield. A lack of ammunition and the setbacks at the brick house and the British camp led Greene to order a general retreat.

The four-hour Battle of Eutaw Springs was a very bloody conflict that resulted in great losses for both sides. Approximately 40 percent of the British force and 25 percent of the Southern Army were casualties. The redcoats had won another Pyrrhic victory. Much as at Guilford Court House, Hobkirk's Hill, and Ninety-Six, the British were temporarily left in control of the battleground. Strategically, however, Greene was able to withdraw his army intact to fight another day, and the redcoats had suffered such losses that they were forced to abandon the ground they had won and to contract their lines of defense. In fact, in the South the British forces were now primarily concentrated at four coastal ports: Charleston, Savannah, Wilmington, and Yorktown. As Governor Nash had noted to Greene, the Rhode Islander possessed "the peculiar Art of making your Enemies run away from their Victories leaving you master."[8]

The day after the Battle of Eutaw Springs, Admiral de Grasse's French fleet of twenty ships and three thousand soldiers arrived in the Chesapeake Bay. By this time, Cornwallis, who had unsuccessfully chased Lafayette's force through Virginia, had led his army of eight thousand troops to Yorktown, on the coast, which he fortified. In August,

Washington and Rochambeau had led their Franco-American force of thirteen thousand troops to Virginia. In early September, de Grasse's fleet defeated the British fleet that had been sent to prevent the entrapment of Cornwallis's army on the Virginia peninsula. When the British fleet limped back to New York and Admiral de Barras's French squadron arrived from Rhode Island, it was clear that there was no escape for Cornwallis's army. In an era of premodern communications, the Allies had carried out an unprecedented campaign of army and navy coordination. When news arrived at the Southern Army's headquarters that the Allies had Cornwallis trapped at Yorktown, Greene reflected on his own reputation as he enviously wrote to Henry Knox, "We have been beating the bush and . . . General [Washington] has come to catch the bird. Never was there a more inviting object to glory. The General is a most fortunate Man, and may success and laurels attend him. We have fought frequently and bled freely, and little glory comes to our share. Our force has been so small that nothing capital could be effected, and our operations have been conducted under every disadvantage that could embarrass either a General or an Army." On October 19, 1781, after suffering through weeks of the Allies' artillery bombardment and suffering numerous casualties, Cornwallis surrendered his entire army.[9]

Greene hoped that after Cornwallis's surrender the French fleet would provide assistance against Charleston. But de Grasse refused to remain in North American waters, citing weather and strategic considerations. Failing to get a blockade of Charleston, Greene went to Charlotte, North Carolina, where he had only limited success in obtaining militia. With fewer than one thousand soldiers fit for duty at the end of October, Greene declared to Washington, "We can attempt nothing further except in the partizan way. . . . I look forward with pain to December, when the whole Virginia line will leave us." Nevertheless, the possibility that the French fleet might return induced the British to abandon Wilmington, and the surrender of Cornwallis's army meant that Virginia and North Carolina might send reinforcements to Greene, who now led a small force of infantry and cavalry against the enemy outpost at Dorchester, South Carolina, in order to protect the area south of the Edisto River. Believing that Greene was leading a much larger force, the enemy commander, after a brief skirmish, abandoned the outpost on December 1 and withdrew his 850 troops to Charleston, where the British prepared for an attack that never occurred. Triumphantly, Greene wrote to Richard Henry Lee "that by a bold manoeuvre we have obliged the enemy to retire to the capital of this State. . . . Thus the conquerors of the Southern World are pent up with little more than ground enough to encamp on." A week later, after a difficult march through the most forbidding swamps Greene had encountered in South Carolina, he had the Southern Army establish a new camp at Round O, approximately thirty-five miles from Charleston.[10]

As the British forces retreated to the coast, Greene recommended that the southern governors treat the defeated loyalists with moderation to avoid initiating a new round of violence. Also by this time, Greene had been informed that some members of Congress were recommending the Rhode Islander for the new position of secretary of war. But Greene was not interested. He did not want to deal with the political aspects of such a position. Greene additionally believed that he must remain in command of the Southern Army until the war was finished in the South. And he knew that when the war ended he would need to make money to pay off his large debts; government service would not be lucrative enough. In the end, Congress did not select Greene as secretary of war; instead, it selected Benjamin Lincoln for the position.

Not long after the Southern Army arrived at Round O, a rumor reached the American camp that perhaps as many as five thousand British troops would be arriving at Charleston. Despite Greene's urgent request, Rochambeau would only send a corps of cavalry to join the Southern Army. And Washington would send only a small number of troops to South Carolina, because he was unsure of Clinton's intentions toward Virginia. Therefore, Greene asked Governor Rutledge and the South Carolina legislature to raise four regiments of African-American troops who should be given their freedom and "treated in all respects as other soldiers; without which, they will be unfit for the duty expected from them." Greene strongly asserted, "That they would make good Soldiers I have not the least doubt and I am persuaded the State has it not in its power to give sufficient reinforcements without incorporating them, either to secure the country, if the

Enemy mean to act vigorously upon an offensive plan, or furnish a force to dispossess them of Charlestown." South Carolina's bias against African-American troops, however, was so great that Greene's proposition was rejected. But the Rhode Islander was able to pay four hundred African Americans to serve as laborers, servants, and wagoners. Moreover, on January 4, 1782, Wayne's Pennsylvania Line and St. Clair's Maryland and Delaware troops arrived at Round O.[11]

At the beginning of January, despite his army being in a wretched condition from a lack of supplies, Greene forced the British to evacuate Johns Island to prevent them from disrupting the South Carolina assembly, which would soon be meeting at nearby Jacksonborough. Several weeks later the legislature resolved that Greene should be ranked with the greatest generals of history and that he be given a plantation confiscated from the loyalists worth ten thousand guineas. The legislature eventually decided to give Greene an estate called Boone's Barony, which had been owned by a former royal governor. Several months later, the North Carolina and Georgia legislatures also voted him gifts of land for his services. North Carolina gave him twenty-five thousand acres in what is now Tennessee, and Georgia gave him a two thousand–acre estate, named Mulberry Grove, that had been confiscated from a loyalist. The plantation, which had some of the best rice-producing land in the South, would become his home after the war. Greene was grateful for the gifts, which he believed would compensate him for his expenditures during the conflict and help give him a fresh start in the postwar period.

In late March, after the South Carolina assembly had adjourned, Greene moved his army near Dorchester to be closer to his provisions. At this time his beloved wife, Caty, whom he had not seen in more than a year, arrived at the headquarters of the Southern Army after a five-month journey from Rhode Island.

Greene's army, however, continued to suffer from numerous problems. He commented on the deplorable hospital facilities, where "numbers of brave fellows, who have bled in the Cause of their Country, have been eat[en] up with maggots & perished in that miserable situation." To Robert Morris, the superintendent of finance in the Articles of Confederation government, he declared that the soldiers "are literally naked, and . . . unless this Army receive[s] pay before the

sickly season approaches it will cease to exist." Moreover, as he informed John Hanson, the president of the Confederation Congress,
"The temper and disposition of the Army for want of clothing, pay,
spirits, and more regular subsistence has given a very discontented
tone to it." Indeed, under these conditions, desertion and mutiny
threatened the army. Knowing that Pennsylvania soldiers, some of
whom had orchestrated a mutiny at Morristown in January 1781,
were now inciting troops in the Southern Army to mutiny, Greene
made preparations to catch the ringleaders red-handed and make ex-
amples of them. Later Greene asserted, "It was talked pretty freely
among the men, that if pay and clothing did not arrive by such a day,
they would march their officers to Dorchester, and allow them only a
few days more, before they would deliver them up to the enemy, unless their grievances were redressed." In April this led to the arrest of
one of the plotters, who was a British deserter, and his execution before the entire army. Others involved in the plot, including Greene's
steward, were sent to Salisbury, where they faced the disgrace of making cartridges. Soldiers knew that now even the suspicion of muti-
nous intentions could lead to this type of sentence. As a result, the
short-term danger of additional rebellious actions had been ended. "I
am confident," Greene asserted, "that nothing but the greatest decision prevented the dreadfull misfortune of a very considerable, if not
a total mutiny."[12]

Despite averting a rebellion in the ranks, Greene during the summer of 1782 saw hundreds of soldiers in his army die from malaria. In
fact, so many died that in late August Greene informed the army that
"the custom of beating the *dead march* at Soldiers funerals, has a ten-
dency to depress the Spirits of the Sick in camp," and therefore he
ordered that "in [the] future this practice be discontinued." Still, as
peace negotiations continued in Paris, Greene turned down General
Leslie's proposal to declare a truce, since he felt he could only accept
this when authorized by Congress. And he did not believe the United
States should accept a truce unless France gave its consent.

Soon thereafter Sir Guy Carleton, who had replaced Clinton as
commander of British forces in North America, ordered Leslie to evacuate St. Augustine and Savannah, and on August 2 Leslie was ordered
to evacuate Charleston as soon as possible. But the British evacuation,

which included approximately 3,800 loyalists and 5,000 slaves, did not begin until early October and was not completed until mid-December. At 11:00 a.m. on December 14 the British rear guard, followed by American troops, marched toward Gadsden's dock and boarded the last transports. About four hours later, Greene and the governor of South Carolina led more Continental troops into Charleston, and they were met by a large and receptive crowd. Without French assistance, the Southern Army had forced the British to evacuate the Carolinas. Earlier Greene had declared to Gen. George Weedon, "My wishes are compleat. It was my pride to get rid of the enemy without foreign aid. I am fond of an alliance, but I wish for the honor of America that liberty may effect her own deliverance."[13]

In January 1783, Nathanael and Caty Greene, along with some guards and members of the general's staff, traveled to Savannah, which the British had evacuated in July. Their short visit allowed state officials to pay tribute to the leader of the American liberators as he inspected the city. The Georgia legislature proclaimed that this "annal in The History of our Country" must "endear the name of Green[e] as long as the Remembrance of british tyranny shall be handed to Posterity." [14]

Greene also used the visit to urge the Georgia legislature to support the proposed federal tax on imports. By October 1782, only Georgia and Rhode Island had not ratified it. But under the Articles of Confederation, a unanimous vote of the states was required in the national congress for a tax to be imposed. Indicating his nationalistic sentiments, Greene wrote to Georgia's governor, "Had not you better submit to the inconveniences of a small tax than to suffer Government to expire and the Army disband. These must be the consequences of a want of revenue. To expect the continuance of either without support is to hope without reason and to expose our cause to enevetable ruin."[15]

Moreover, the trip to Savannah offered the Greenes an opportunity to visit Mulberry Grove, which was the plantation fourteen miles north of the city that had been given to the general. Although the plantation had been badly neglected during the war, the Greenes were impressed with the large two-story Georgian house, and they now began to give serious consideration to the plantation as their postwar home. Greene certainly believed that the postwar South would offer a great opportunity for gaining the wealth that he wanted. Nearly a year earlier, he had stated, "This Country affords a fine field for making a fortune."[16]

By January Greene had sent the 1,400 soldiers in his army to James Island, near Charleston, where they established a winter camp that provided an abundant supply of water, wild fowl, fish, and shellfish to supplement their meager supplies. Indeed, a shortage of provisions had continued to be a major problem for the Southern Army. In October, however, Robert Morris, the superintendent of finance in the Articles of Confederation government, had authorized Greene to use private contractors to provide supplies to the troops. But the only person willing to provide provisions was John Banks, a merchant with the firm of Hunter, Banks & Company in Fredericksburg, Virginia, who had a reputation for shady transactions. Soon a private letter by Banks was made public, in which he claimed to have established business alliances with Robert Forsyth, a key subordinate of Greene, and Ichabod Burnet, Greene's most trusted military aide. In the letter Banks also bragged that Greene had given him special treatment in exchange for a place in Banks's firm after the war.

Greene immediately denied Banks's assertion that he had given special consideration to the contractor, and he swore an oath before a judge that he had no private connection to Hunter, Banks & Company. In addition, he had Banks publicly confirm this. But rumors of such a connection had spread through the army and were believed by many because Greene had alienated a number of cavalry officers in the summer and fall of 1782 when he had ended the customary practice of allowing cavalry officers to sell for personal profit any of the horses they had confiscated for military use. The cavalry officers now asserted that Greene, who had already been rewarded by the southern legislatures, was also profiting from an arrangement with Banks while denying the officers their just financial rewards. In short, Greene's reputation, which he had done so much to promote, was now under intense attack within the army.

Nevertheless, Greene continued to use Banks's services, and he maintained ties to Burnet and Forsyth. This seemingly odd behavior can perhaps be partly explained as resulting from his friendship with

Forsyth and Burnet. More importantly, however, Greene continued to experience difficulties as he tried to find another company to provide needed supplies to the army. But in April 1783, when Greene pledged his bond as financial security for Banks's purchases, he compounded his problems, since Banks's company was having difficulties with creditors and Banks did not save money from transactions to cover Greene's bond. Instead, he invested the money in speculative business ventures in a failed attempt to save Hunter, Banks & Company. As a result, the company's creditors demanded that Greene reimburse them for their losses, which totaled about thirty thousand pounds sterling. This debt would threaten to drive him into bankruptcy.

On April 23 the Southern Army was officially informed that peace terms had been reached between the United States and Great Britain. To Secretary of War Lincoln, Greene declared, "The terms are so honorable and so interesting to the United States that every heart must over flow with gratitude upon the occasion. A revolution so important in its object and terminated with so much success is singular in the history of mankind considering the physical and political difficulties which have attended the dispute. Liberty and property secure and our independence acknowledged nothing remains but to conduct our Government upon constitutional principles to render us respectable abroad and happy at home." Greene, however, had already expressed his fear that the states would not relinquish to the national government the needed authority for establishing the United States on a sound basis.[17]

Many soldiers now eagerly desired to leave the South as soon as possible to avoid the malarial season. In fact, a number of troops in the Maryland Line, asserting that their terms of enlistment had expired, decided to leave the American camp. In response, Greene rode to where the mutineers had gathered and ordered them to return to their quarters, which most did. But nine days later, some one hundred dragoons of the Virginia cavalry's First Regiment deserted en masse and headed for their home state. Desperately wanting to prevent other mutinies, Greene agreed to advance a month's pay to the army's remaining dragoons in Lee's Legion and he allowed them to bid for their own horses with money diverted from their pay. This, however, outraged the Legion's infantry since they would not benefit. Fearing a mutiny by the infantry, Greene granted them a month's pay, which quieted their anger. Around June 1, however, the Maryland Continentals again seemed on the verge of mutiny. And soon the feelings of discontent had spread to the Virginia Line. Acting swiftly, Greene jailed the leader of the dissatisfied troops and brought the rest of the army to battle formation, which quelled the nascent insurrection.

Nevertheless, as the soldiers watchfully waited in June for the transports that would take them home, their fear of fever continued to grow. As a result, many began to desert, and Greene feared that if the ships did not arrive soon the entire army would decide to leave on its own. To keep his troops together until all of the transports arrived, Greene stated on June 21 in his orders to the Southern Army that it was "his happiness . . . [to have] had the honor to command an army no less distinguished for its patience than bravery. . . . United by principle and cemented by affection, you have exhibited to the world a proof, that elevated souls and persevering tempers will triumph over every difficulty. . . . Our great object is answered; our first wish obtained." And Greene asserted, "Hostilities having ceased, and a general peace almost concluded, it only remains to complete your character, that you retire from that field with Propriety, where you have acted with Glory." On June 21 the first transport arrived and by July 29 all of the soldiers had left Charleston; but Greene temporarily remained. "I am left," he declared, "like Samson after Delilah cut his locks."[18]

Caty, anxious to get back to their children, had taken the first vessel that had left with troops for Philadelphia, but once there she had made purchases totaling six hundred pounds sterling that Greene could not afford at that time. Finally, on August 11, Greene, who had decided to travel overland, began the journey northward. In Virginia, however, Greene's carriage overturned, and he barely escaped death or serious injury by lifting the carriage being dragged by the horse and letting it pass over him. During his travels northward, he received tributes in several towns, and in early October he was reunited with George Washington at Trenton, where years before they had led American troops to a stunning victory.

On October 7 the triumphant Greene and Washington proceeded to Princeton where the Articles of Confederation Congress was in session. The Congress had again abandoned Philadelphia, but this time its exile was due to American, not British, troops. Disgruntled American soldiers, mostly from Pennsylvania, had marched on Philadelphia to force the Congress to give them their back pay. Having relocated to Princeton, the Congress received the commander in chief of the Continental Army and the commander of the Southern Department. The Congress awarded two captured brass cannons to Greene in recognition of his service and granted his request to visit his family in Rhode Island. However Greene first went to New York City, which the British evacuated on November 25. But he did not stay for Washington's emotional farewell to his officers at Fraunces Tavern on December 4. Eager to be reunited with his family, Greene embarked for home after more than eight years in the service of his country. His military career was now behind him.

Aftermath (1783–86)

O N NOVEMBER 27 Greene arrived in Newport, where he was greeted by a large and exuberant crowd. More importantly, he was reunited with his family. Indeed, Greene now saw his entire family together for the first time. Though initially shy, the children soon became closely attached to their father. Years later Cornelia Greene remembered that he "was our boon companion and playfellow who winked at every atrocity we perpetrated." And many of the Greenes' friends, including Lafayette and Steuben, visited them. The family settled into a renovated house in town, and here Caty gave birth to their fifth child, named Louisa. But as Greene's family grew, so did his financial problems. His old quartermaster accounts were still unsettled and Congress might demand payment. Greene also found out that a large investment he had made in 1779 in Barnabas Deane and Company was now worth less than one-tenth of its original amount. More importantly, creditors were pursuing him because of the notes he had signed for Banks. Filled with anxiety for his family and himself, Greene complained to Caty, "I never owned so much property as now, and yet never felt so poor and unhappy."[1]

As he assessed his financial problems and sought ways of alleviating them, Greene turned to several business ventures. Although his shipping concern with his brothers had lost a significant amount of money, he made plans with Jacob and his cousin Griffin for opening a shipping line between Charleston and the West Indies. In addition, he began to operate his two plantations, Mulberry Grove in Georgia and Boone's Barony in South Carolina, especially for growing rice. This, however, added substantial expenses, as he was required to purchase tools, seed, livestock, and many slaves. Although he had been opposed to the institution of slavery—partly a reflection of his Quaker upbringing—he now felt compelled to make use of slave labor to develop his plantations. To justify this, he argued that the slaves would be better off under his care. Thus, Greene, like many other American leaders during the Revolutionary era, ironically waged a war for freedom while continuing to uphold the institution of slavery. But the rice crops in 1783 and 1784 did not meet expectations, in part because of a hurricane in the latter year that destroyed half of the crop at Boone's Barony.

After refusing an appointment in 1784 to a commission to negotiate treaties with Indian tribes, he did travel to Philadelphia for the inaugural meeting of the Society of the Cincinnati, which was an elite organization for Continental Army officers and their descendants. In addition, as a result of an indenture from John Banks and one of his partners for a large undivided half share of land, Greene acquired ownership of thousands of acres of very fertile land on Cumberland Island and Little Cumberland Island off the coast of Georgia. The oak and pine trees alone were estimated to be worth forty thousand pounds sterling. To begin logging operations, however, he would have to somehow find additional funds. Even so, Greene clearly believed he needed to borrow more money for investments in the short run to avoid bankruptcy in the long run. From early 1784 to early 1786 he tried to obtain a loan in Europe, but European lenders were reluctant to provide loans on account of the poor condition of America's postwar economy and the failure of the Articles of Confederation government to begin paying off the nation's debts. Moreover, as he unsuccessfully tried to obtain a loan in Europe, Greene gave Jeremiah Wadsworth the power of attorney to sell several thousand acres of his land in New York and New Jersey. Prospective buyers, however, did not believe the lands were worth the approximately two thousand pounds sterling that Greene had stated was their combined value. Depressed and dismayed by his financial problems, he wrote to Caty, "I tremble at my own situation, when I think of the enormous sums I owe and the great difficulty of obtaining Money."[2]

In August, Greene requested that Richard Henry Lee petition the Articles of Confederation Congress to have the national government pay for the debts Greene had incurred on behalf of the Continental Army. Greene declared that he should have earlier laid the issue before Congress, but he had hoped to pay off the debts without its intervention. Since this had not occurred, Greene prophetically asserted, "[A]s life is uncertain, I should do great injustice to my family not to lay the matter before" the national legislature. It would be seven years, however, before Congress acted on his request. In 1786 Greene noted to his old friend Henry Knox that he faced problems everywhere he looked. "My family," he stated, "is in distress and I am overwhelmed with difficulties and God knows when or where they will end." This was not the postwar world that he had envisioned for his family or his reputation.[3]

Greene also suffered another assault on his reputation when James Gunn, a former cavalry officer in the Revolutionary War, challenged him to a duel. In 1782 Greene had accused Gunn of taking a horse from the Continental Army. This had led to a court of inquiry, which cleared Gunn of any wrongdoing. Greene, however, did not accept the court's finding, and he subsequently got Congress to pass a resolution supporting his action against Gunn. By 1785 Greene considered Gunn mentally disturbed and he noted that a commanding officer could not be answerable to every soldier who felt offended in some way during the war. Therefore, Greene refused Gunn's challenge, a decision applauded by Washington and Greene's other close friends. Washington, in particular, asserted that Greene's "honor and reputation" were completely upheld by his decision to reject the challenge. But Gunn vowed to kill Greene by other means, so Greene now carried a weapon for his personal protection.[4]

To add to Nathanael's and Caty's miseries, their most recent child, a daughter named Catharine, who had been born in August 1785, died later that month of whooping cough. As their depression after her death lingered on, Greene in October moved his family to Georgia.

After the long trip on violent seas to the bustling port of Savannah, the family recuperated in the town for several weeks. In November they made the fourteen-mile trip up the Savannah River to their Mulberry Grove plantation. Caty was once again enamored of the estate's two-story Georgian home. In addition to this house, the plantation had stables, a coach house, a poultry house, and several other buildings. Soon many friends were stopping by to visit the general and his vivacious wife. The most frequent visitor was Anthony Wayne, who had been awarded a plantation on the Savannah River adjacent to Greene's. But in April 1786 heartache occurred again when Caty, pregnant with her seventh child, fell in the kitchen and went into labor. The baby was born prematurely and soon died.

By this time Greene was also increasingly concerned about the future of the United States. Since the national government under the Articles of Confederation did not have the power to raise revenue through taxation, he felt the nation was in danger of breaking apart. He asserted, "Many people secretly wish that every State should be completely independent, and that, as soon as our public debts are liquidated, Congress should be no more—a plan that would be as fatal to our happiness at home as it would be ruinous to our interest abroad." To prevent this, he advocated the creation of a national government that would have increased power. Greene had already offered an analysis of the situation in 1780. He rejected the idea that the appointment of a dictator was the best solution. Instead, he declared, "Call a convention of the States and establish a Congress upon a constitutional footing. Give them full powers to govern the empire." But by 1786 Greene and like-minded nationalists were still unable to get all of the state legislatures to support this change.[5]

Despite his financial problems, in the spring of 1786 Greene was optimistic about that year's crops at Mulberry Grove. He noted to a friend that nearly two hundred acres of rice and corn had been planted. But he was most proud of the family's garden. "The fruit trees and flowering shrubs," he bragged, "form a pleasing variety. We have . . . as fine Lettice as you ever saw. The mocking-birds surround us evening and morning. The weather is mild, and the vegetable kingdom progressing to perfection. . . . We have in the same orchard apples, pears, peaches, & apricots, nectarines, plumbs of different kinds, figs, pomegranates, and oranges. And we have strawberries which measure three inches round."[6]

On June 12, Greene and Caty went to Savannah to meet with one of Greene's creditors, E. John Collett, at the home of Nathaniel Pendleton, who had been Greene's aide during the war and was now a lawyer who was helping his former commanding officer with legal matters stemming from John Banks's debts. Having failed to get Congress to pay for the debts he had guaranteed to Banks and others as contractors during the war, Greene now agreed to sign new bonds for the money he owed Collett. As Nathanael and Caty proceeded back to Mulberry Grove, they visited with a neighbor, William Gibbons, and Greene spent a very hot day inspecting Gibbons's rice fields. Following supper, the Greenes continued on their journey. But Greene began to complain of a severe headache, and by the time they reached home the pain had significantly increased. By the next day he was especially suffering from great pain above the eyes and there was some swelling in that area. By the evening Greene had fallen into a semi-stupor. As doctors bled him and applied blisters during the next thirty-six hours, Greene's condition worsened. His entire head became swelled and appeared inflamed. At approximately 6:00 a.m. on June 19 Greene, who was five weeks short of his forty-fourth birthday, died while his beloved Caty and some friends, including Anthony Wayne, grieved nearby. Wayne, who was devastated by the death of his old comrade-in-arms, wrote to Col. Henry Jackson, "My dear friend General Greene is no more. . . . He was great as a soldier, greater as a citizen, immaculate as a friend. . . . I have seen a great and good man die."[7]

Friends dressed Greene's body in the uniform that he had worn on formal occasions as a major general in the Continental Army. The next day his body was taken down the river to Savannah. The ships in the harbor flew their flags at half-mast, and the stores in the town were closed to honor the memory of Greene. As a band played a solemn dirge, a long procession, in which members of the Society of the Cincinnati participated, took the casket to be interred in a vault following an Episcopalian funeral service and the firing of salutes. Two weeks after the funeral, the Articles of Confederation Congress voted to place a statue in the nation's capital in honor of Greene. It would take nearly a century, however, before the monument of Greene was erected, in Stanton Park in Washington, D.C. A few years earlier the state of Rhode Island provided another statue of Greene for the National Hall of Statuary in the Capitol at Washington. But in 1829 the people of Savannah had already constructed an obelisk at Johnson Square to remember Greene's distinguished military service in the South. During his visit to the United States in 1825, Lafayette had laid the cornerstone of this monument. Eventually, however, there developed confusion over the location of Greene's body. At the turn of the twentieth century the Rhode Island Society of the Cincinnati located the remains of Greene in the "Jones" vault in Savannah's Colonial Park Cemetery. Near Greene's remains were those of a male in his late teens, which were presumed to be those of Greene's son, George Washington Greene, who drowned in 1793. The remains of both were moved to the Johnson Square memorial in 1902.

Greene had left a widow with five young children and a great financial debt. Congress would eventually—in 1792 and 1796—pay the $47,504 that Greene owed on Banks's debts. Nevertheless, Caty would sell Boone's Barony in 1796 to cover other family debts. Despite the loss of her husband and the economic problems, she would remain at Mulberry Grove. To educate her children, Caty would hire tutors, including Eli Whitney in 1793. Aware of Whitney's mechanical talents, she urged him to develop a means for quickly separating upland (short-staple) cotton from its seed. He soon invented the cotton gin, which would make upland cotton a profitable crop and thus expand the cotton belt of the South over vast inland areas where long-staple cotton, with its easier-to-separate seeds, would not grow.

Nathanael Greene journeyed far in his abbreviated life, and in the process the former Quaker emerged as America's most innovative general during the Revolutionary War. Serving throughout the conflict, he became a major architect of the American victory. And having distinguished himself as a defender of the nation's independence, Greene would gain the enduring heroic fame that he had pursued across all the trying years of war.

Notes

Note: In keeping with the format of the *Military Profiles* series, the endnotes provide only the sources of quotations.

Chapter 1
1. Nathanael Greene to Samuel Ward Jr., October 9, 1772, in *The Papers of General Nathanael Greene,* edited by Richard K. Showman, et al., 13 vols. (Chapel Hill: The University of North Carolina Press, 1976–2005) 1:47–49. Hereafter cited as *PGNG*.
2. Nathanael Greene to Samuel Ward Jr., September 26, 1771, in *PGNG*, 1:23.
3. Nathanael Greene to Samuel Ward Jr., January 25, 1773, in *PGNG*, 1:53. Eyewitness descriptions make it appear very likely that Nathanael Greene's cousin, Rufus Greene, captain of the captured ship *Fortune*, was among those who burned the *Gaspee*.
4. "Subscription," August 29, 1774, in *PGNG*, 1:67.

Chapter 2
1. Nathanael Greene to James M. Varnum, October 31, 1774, in *PGNG*, 1:75–76; Nathanael Greene to Samuel Ward Sr., December 18, 1775, in *PGNG*, 1:163; Nathanael Greene to Samuel Ward Sr., October 23, 1775, in *PGNG*, 1:140.
2. Nathanael Greene to James M. Varnum, October 31, 1774, in *PGNG*, 1:75.
3. Nathanael Greene to Catharine Greene, June 2, 1775, in *PGNG*, 1:83.
4. Nathanael Greene to Catharine Greene, quoted in Theodore Thayer, *Nathanael Greene: Strategist of the American Revolution* (New York: Twayne Publishers, 1960), 58; Nathanael Greene to Nicholas Cooke, June 18, 1775, in *PGNG*, 1:87. The Army of Observation also had a company of artillery.

5. Nathanael Greene to Samuel Ward Sr., July 14, 1775, in *PGNG*, 1:99. Greene later described Washington as "a great and a good man," and wished him "immortal honnor." Nathanael Greene to Samuel Ward Sr., December 18, 1775, in *PGNG*, 1:163.

6. Nathanael Greene to Catharine Greene, August 27, 1775, in *PGNG*, 1:111.

7. Nathanael Greene to Jacob Greene, February 8, 1776, in *PGNG*, 1:193.

Chapter 3

1. Nathanael Greene to Nicholas Cooke, September 12, 1775, in *PGNG*, 1:119; Nathanael Greene to Samuel Ward, Sr., October 23, 1775, in *PGNG*, 1:140; Nathanael Greene to Jacob Greene, December 20, 1775, in *PGNG*, 1:167; Nathanael Greene to Samuel Ward, Sr., January 4, 1776, in *PGNG*, 1:176.

2. Nathanael Greene to John Adams, July 14, 1776, in *PGNG*, 1:256.

3. Nathanael Greene to Jacob Greene, August 30, 1776, in *PGNG*, 1:291. John Adams and Henry Knox later asserted that Greene's presence on Long Island would have prevented the disaster.

4. Nathanael Greene to George Washington, September 5, 1776, in *PGNG*, 1:295. Washington had asked Congress to permit the destruction of the city, if it had to be evacuated. But Congress had stated that all care should be taken to prevent damage to the city.

5. Nathanael Greene to Henry Knox, quoted in Thayer, *Nathanael Greene*, 122.

6. George Washington to John Augustine Washington, quoted in Don Higginbotham, *The War of American Independence: Military Attitudes, Policies, and Practice, 1763–1789* (New York: The Macmillan Company, 1971), 165.

7. Nathanael Greene to John Hancock, December 21, 1776, in *PGNG*, 1:370; Thomas Paine's "The American Crisis," quoted in George F. Scheer and Hugh F. Rankin, *Rebels and Redcoats* (Cleveland and New York: The World Publishing Company, 1957), 210.

Chapter 4

1. Nathanael Greene to John Hancock, December 21, 1776, in *PGNG*, 1:372. In a strict sense, however, Greene was not advocating dictatorial powers since he declared that Congress would reserve to itself the right to confirm or repeal Washington's measures. Furthermore, the success at Trenton and Princeton would help con-

vince the Congress to grant Washington the increased authority that Greene advocated.

2. Sullivan, St. Clair, Washington, and Biddle quoted in David Hackett Fischer, *Washington's Crossing* (New York: Oxford University Press, 2004), 225–62, 516; Nathanael Greene to Catharine Greene, December 30, 1776, in *PGNG*, 1:377. James Monroe, however, almost became a fatality. A Hessian musket ball severed an artery in the future president and he began to bleed profusely. A New Jersey physician, who had joined Monroe's company just the night before, clamped the artery to prevent the Virginian from bleeding to death.

3. Nathanael Greene as quoted in Thayer, *Nathanael Greene*, 147.

4. Nathanael Greene to Henry Marchant, July [25?], 1778, in *PGNG*, 2:471.

5. Nathanael Greene to Catharine Greene, September 14, 1777, in *PGNG*, 2:162.

6. Nathanael Greene to James McHenry, July 24, 1781, in *PGNG*, 9:74.

7. Nathaniel Greene to Henry Lee, February 18, 1782, in *PGNG*, 10:379; Nathanael Greene to Henry Marchant, July [25?], 1778, in *PGNG*, 2:471.

8. Nathanael Greene to John Clark Jr., November 5, 1777, in *PGNG*, 2:191.

9. Joseph Plumb Martin quoted in Scheer and Rankin, *Rebels and Redcoats*, 249.

10. Nathanael Greene to George Washington, November 24, 1777, in *PGNG*, 2:209; Nathanael Greene to George Washington, November 24, 1777, in *PGNG*, 2:211.

Chapter 5

1. Benjamin Rush quoted in Thayer, *Nathanael Greene*, 215; Nathanael Greene to Alexander McDougall, January 25, 1778, in *PGNG*, 2:260.

2. Nathanael Greene to Alexander McDougall, January 25 and March 28, 1778, in *PGNG*, 2:259, 326.

3. Nathanael Greene to Thomas McKean, June 3, 1778, in *PGNG*, 2:424; Thomas McKean to Nathanael Greene, June 9, 1778, in *PGNG*, 2:430.

4. Nathanael Greene to George Washington, June 18 and June 24, 1778, in *PGNG*, 2:440, 447.

5. James McHenry to John Cox, July 1, 1778, quoted in Scheer and Rankin, *Rebels and Redcoats*, 333.

6. Nathanael Greene to George Washington, July 21, 1778, in *PGNG*, 2:461; George Washington to Nathanael Greene, July 21, 1778, in *PGNG*, 2:464.

7. Nathanael Greene to John Brown, September 6, 1778, in *PGNG*, 2:511.

8. Nathanael Greene to James Duane, April 16, 1779, in *PGNG*, 3:412.

9. Nathanael Greene quoted in Thayer, *Nathanael Greene*, 262; Nathanael Greene to Samuel B. Webb, December 21, 1779, in *PGNG*, 5:194.

10. Nathanael Greene to John Jay, April 27, 1779, in *PGNG*, 3:432; Nathanael Greene to George Washington, April 24, 1779, in *PGNG*, 3:426–27; Nathanael Greene to James Duane, April 16, 1779, in *PGNG*, 3:412. Greene's concern about his reputation was in keeping with the belief in Revolutionary America that an individual needed to defend honor to have a respected place in society.

11. Nathanael Greene to Moore Furman, January 4, 1780, in *PGNG*, 5:230; Joseph Plumb Martin quoted in *PGNG*, 5:237; Nathanael Greene to Benoni Hathaway, January 6, 1780, in *PGNG*, 5:243; Nathanael Greene quoted in James Thomas Flexner, *George Washington in the American Revolution, 1775–1783* (Boston and Toronto: Little, Brown, 1967), 355.

12. Nathanael Greene to George Washington, March 8–12, 1780, in *PGNG*, 5:450.

13. Nathanael Greene to Alexander McDougall, April 15, 1780, in *PGNG*, 5:520.

14. Nathanael Greene to Jonathan Trumbull, May 7, 1780, in *PGNG*, 5:548–49.

15. Nathanael Greene to William Greene, May 27, 1780, in *PGNG*, 5:582.

16. Nathanael Greene to Jeremiah Wadsworth, July 10, 1780, in *PGNG*, 6:78.

17. Nathanael Greene to John Davis, July 9, 1780, in *PGNG*, 6:74; Nathanael Greene to Joseph Reed, August 29, 1780, in *PGNG*, 6:243.

18. Nathanael Greene to Samuel Huntington, July 26, 1780, in *PGNG*, 6:157.

19. Nathanael Greene to Catharine Greene, August 14, 1780, in *PGNG*, 6:212.

20. Nathanael Greene to Griffin Greene, September 29, 1780, in *PGNG*, 6:322.

21. Nathanael Greene to Nathaniel Peabody, September 6, 1780, in *PGNG*, 6:267; Nathanael Greene to Alexander Hamilton, January 10, 1781, in *PGNG*, 7:90. In the statement to Hamilton, Greene was drawing on ideas from David Hume's essay titled "Of the Love of Fame."

22. George Washington to the President of Congress, October 22, 1780, and George Washington to John Mathews, October 23, 1780, in *The Writings of George Washington, from the Original Manuscript Sources, 1745–1799*, edited by John C. Fitzpatrick, 39 vols., (Washington, DC: Government Printing Office, 1931–1944), 20:244, 249; Robert Howe to Abner Nash, October 23, 1780, quoted in Hugh F. Rankin, *The North Carolina Continentals* (Chapel Hill: University of North Carolina Press, 1971), 259; George Washington to Nathanael Greene, October 22, 1780, in *PGNG*, 6:424.

Chapter 6

1. Nathanael Greene to George Washington, November 19, 1780, in *PGNG*, 6:488–89; Nathanael Greene to Catharine Greene, October 15 or 16, 1780, in *PGNG*, 6:398.

2. Nathanael Greene quoted in Higginbotham, *The War of American Independence*, 365; Nathanael Greene to Samuel Huntington, October 27, 1780, in *PGNG*, 6:436; Nathanael Greene quoted in Scheer and Rankin, *Rebels and Redcoats*, 423.

3. Nathanael Greene to Joseph Reed, January 9, 1781, quoted in Rankin, *The North Carolina Continentals*, 262.

4. Nathanael Greene to Thomas Jefferson, December 6, 1780, in *PGNG*, 6:530.

5. Soldier quoted in Rankin, *The North Carolina Continentals*, 263.

6. Alexander Martin to Abner Nash, December 21, 1780, quoted in Rankin, *The North Carolina Continentals*, 262. This letter is dated December 25, 1780, in *PGNG*, 6:575.

7. Nathanael Greene to Thomas Sumter, January 8, 1781, in *PGNG*, 7:74–75; Nathanael Greene to Francis Marion, December 4, 1780, in *PGNG*, 6:520.

8. Nathanael Greene to Thomas Burke, August 25, 1781, in *PGNG*, 9:237. Regarding his strategy in the South, Greene asserted, "[T]here are few Generals that has run oftner, or more lustily than I have done, But I have taken care not to run too farr; and commonly have run as fast forward as backward, to convince our Enemy that

we were like a Crab, that could run either way." Nathanael Greene to Jeremiah Wadsworth, July 18, 1781, *PGNG*, 9: 41. Two centuries later, Mao Tse-tung described this type of strategy thus: "Enemy advances, we retreat; enemy halts, we harass; enemy tires, we attack; enemy retreats, we pursue." Mao Tse-tung quoted in Russell F. Weigley, *The American Way of War: A History of United States Strategy and Policy* (Bloomington: Indiana University Press, 1973), 36. Russell Weigley himself has written, "The later course of American military history, featuring a rapid rise from poverty of resources to plenty, cut short any further American evolution of Greene's type of strategy. He therefore remains alone as an American master developing a strategy of unconventional warfare." *The American Way of War*, 36.

9. Nathanael Greene to Daniel Morgan, December 29, 1780, in *PGNG*, 7:22; Nathanael Greene quoted in Rankin, *The North Carolina Continentals*, 266.

10. Nathanael Greene to George Washington, January 13, 1781, in *PGNG*, 7:111; Nathanael Greene quoted in Rankin, *The North Carolina Continentals*, 267.

11. Nathanael Greene to Catharine Greene, January 12, 1781, in *PGNG*, 7:102.

12. Nathanael Greene to George Washington, January 24, 1781, in *PGNG*, 7:181; Nathanael Greene to Isaac Huger, January 30, 1781, in *PGNG*, 7:220.

13. Nathanael Greene to Thomas Sumter, February 9, 1781, in *PGNG*, 7:266; Nathanael Greene to Abner Nash, February 9, 1781, in *PGNG*, 7:263.

14. Charles Cornwallis quoted in Scheer and Rankin, *Rebels and Redcoats*, 441; Nathanael Greene to Richard Caswell, February 18, 1781, in *PGNG*, 7:309.

15. Nathanael Greene to Thomas Jefferson, March 10, 1781, in *PGNG*, 7:420; Nathanael Greene to George Washington, March 18, 1781, in *PGNG*, 7:451.

16. Joseph Reed to Nathanael Greene, June 16, 1781, in *PGNG*, 8:397.

17. Nathanael Greene to George Washington, March 29, 1781, in *PGNG*, 7:481.

Chapter 7

1. Nathanael Greene to James Emmet, April 3, 1781, in *PGNG*, 8:33; Nathanael Greene to Thomas Sumter, March 30, 1781, in *PGNG*, 8:12.

2. Nathanael Greene to Joseph Reed, May 4, 1781, in *PGNG*, 8:201.

3. Nathanael Greene to Baron von Steuben, April 27, 1781, in *PGNG*, 8:162; Nathanael Greene to the Chevalier de La Luzerne, April 28, 1781, in *PGNG*, 8:168.

4. Nathanael Greene to Catharine Greene, July 18, 1781, in *PGNG*, 9:36.

5. Nathanael Greene quoted in *PGNG*, 9:xii.

6. Nathanael Greene quoted in Scheer and Rankin, *Rebels and Redcoats*, 461.

7. Greene quoted in Rankin, *The North Carolina Continentals*, 355.

8. Abner Nash to Nathanael Greene, April 7, 1781, in *PGNG*, 8:64.

9. Nathanael Greene to Henry Knox, September 29, 1781, in *PGNG*, 9: 411–12.

10. Nathanael Greene to George Washington, October 25, 1781, in *PGNG*, 9:485; Nathanael Greene to Richard Henry Lee, December 9, 1781, in *PGNG*, 10:16–17.

11. Nathanael Greene to John Rutledge, December 9, 1781, in *PGNG*, 10:22.

12. Nathanael Greene to Thomas McKean, October 25, 1781, in *PGNG*, 9:482; Nathanael Greene to Robert Morris, April 22, 1782, in *PGNG*, 11:94; Nathanael Greene to John Hanson, April 13 and May 18, 1782, in *PGNG*, 11:50, 199; Nathanael Greene to George Washington, May 19, 1782, in *PGNG*, 11:213.

13. General Greene's Orders, August 26, 1782, in *PGNG*, 11:576; Nathanael Greene to George Weedon, October 1, 1782, in *PGNG*, 12:4.

14. "Address of the Georgia Legislature," January 13, 1783, in *PGNG*, 12:373.

15. Nathanael Greene to Lyman Hall, January 20, 1783, in *PGNG*, 12:380.

16. Nathanael Greene to Griffin Greene, April 14, 1782, in *PGNG*, 11:58.

17. Nathanael Greene to Benjamin Lincoln, April 19, 1783, in *PGNG*, 12: 620–21.

18. General Greene's Orders, June 21, 1783, *PGNG*, 13: 44–45; Nathanael Greene to Charles Pettit, July 29, 1783, in *PGNG*, 13:75.

Chapter 8

1. Cornelia Greene quoted in John Stegeman and Janet Stegeman, *Caty: A Biography of Catharine Littlefield Greene* (Providence: Rhode Island Bicentennial Foundation, 1977), 110; Nathanael Greene to Catharine Greene, September 8, 1784, in *PGNG*, 13:387.

2. Nathanael Greene to Catharine Greene, April 14, 1785, in *PGNG*, 13: 493.

3. Nathanael Greene to Richard Henry Lee, August 22, 1785, in *PGNG*, 13: 564; Nathanael Greene to Henry Knox, March 12, 1786, in *PGNG*, 13: 668.

4. George Washington to Nathanael Greene, May 20, 1785, in Fitzpatrick, *The Writings of George Washington*, 28:144.

5. Nathanael Greene quoted in Francis Vinton Greene, *General Greene* (New York: D. Appleton and Company, 1893, reprint ed., Port Washington, New York and London: Kennikat Press, 1970), 309–10.

6. Nathanael Greene to Ethan Clarke, April 6, 1786, in *PGNG*, 13: 676–77.

7. Anthony Wayne to Henry Jackson, quoted in Greene, *General Greene*, 313.

Selected Bibliography

Anderson, Lee Patrick. *Forgotten Patriot: The Life and Times of Major-General Nathanael Greene*. Parkland, Florida: Universal Publishers, 2002.

Black, Jeremy. *War for America: The Fight for Independence, 1775–1783*. New York: St. Martin's Press, 1991.

Carp, E. Wayne. *To Starve the Army at Pleasure: Continental Army Administration and American Political Culture, 1775–1783*. Chapel Hill: University of North Carolina Press, 1984.

Colbourn, Trevor, ed. *Fame and the Founding Fathers*. Indianapolis: Liberty Fund, 1974.

Dederer, John Morgan. *Making Bricks Without Straw: Nathanael Greene's Southern Campaign and Mao Tse-Tung's Mobile War*. Manhattan, Kans.: Sunflower University Press, 1983.

Golway, Terry. *Washington's General: Nathanael Greene and the Triumph of the American Revolution*. New York: Henry Holt, 2005.

Greene, George Washington. *The Life of Nathanael Greene, Major-General in the Army of the Revolution*. 3 vols. New York: G. P. Putnam and Son, 1867–1871.

Haller, Stephen E. *William Washington: Cavalryman of the Revolution*. Bowie, Md.: Heritage Books, 2001.

Higginbotham, Don. *The War of American Independence: Military Attitudes, Policies, and Practice, 1763–1789*. New York: Macmillan, 1971.

Johnson, William. *Sketches of the Life and Correspondence of Nathanael Greene, Major General of the Armies of the United States*. 2 vols. Charleston: Printed for the author by A. E. Miller, 1822.

Lengel, Edward G. *General George Washington: A Military Life*. New York: Random House, 2005.

Martin, James Kirby, and Mark Edward Lender. *A Respectable Army:*

The Military Origins of the Republic, 1763–1789. Arlington Heights, Ill.: Harlan Davidson, 1982.

Middlekauff, Robert. *The Glorious Cause: The American Revolution, 1763–1789*. New York: Oxford University Press, 1985.

Pancake, John S. *This Destructive War: The British Campaigns in the Carolinas, 1780–1782*. Tuscaloosa: University of Alabama Press, 1985.

Rankin, Hugh F. *The North Carolina Continentals*. Chapel Hill: University of North Carolina Press, 1971.

Risch, Erna. *Supplying Washington's Army*. Washington, D.C.: Center of Military History, 1981.

Royster, Charles. *A Revolutionary People at War: The Continental Army and American Character, 1775–1783*. Chapel Hill: University of North Carolina Press, 1979.

Scheer, George F., and Hugh F. Rankin. *Rebels and Redcoats*. Cleveland: World Publishing Company, 1957.

Stegeman, John, and Janet Stegman. *Caty: A Biography of Catharine Littlefield Greene*. Providence: Rhode Island Bicentennial Foundation, 1977.

Thayer, Theodore. *Nathanael Greene: Strategist of the American Revolution*. New York: Twayne Publishers, 1960.

Ward, Christopher. *The War of the Revolution*. 2 vols. New York: Macmillan, 1952.

Ward, Harry W. *The American Revolution: Nationhood Achieved, 1763–1788*. New York: St. Martin's Press, 1995.

Weigley, Russell F. *The Partisan War: The South Carolina Campaign of 1780–1782*. Columbia: University of South Carolina Press, 1970.

Wood, Gordon S. *The American Revolution: A History*. New York: Modern Library, 2003.

Wood, W. J. *Battles of the Revolutionary War, 1775–1781*. New York: Da Capo Press, 1995.

Wright, Robert K. *The Continental Army*. Washington, D.C.: Center of Military History, 1989.

Index

Throughout this index the abbreviation NG is used to indicate Nathanael Greene.

About the Author

Steven E. Siry is a professor at Baldwin-Wallace College in Berea, Ohio. He has also taught at Central Michigan University and the University of Cincinnati, where he received his Ph.D. in history. In addition to journal articles and book chapters, he has written *De Witt Clinton and the American Political Economy: Sectionalism, Politics, and Republican Ideology, 1787– 1828* (1990).